My Heart Sutra

A WORLD IN 260 CHARACTERS

T0161912

OTHER BOOKS BY FREDERIK L. SCHODT

ORIGINAL WORKS

Manga! Manga! The World of Japanese Comics

Inside the Robot Kingdom: Japan, Mechatronics, and the Coming Robotopia

America and the Four Japans: Friend, Foe, Model, Mirror

Dreamland Japan: Writings on Modern Manga

Native American in the Land of the Shogun: Ranald MacDonald and the Opening of Japan

The Astro Boy Essays: Osamu Tezuka, Mighty Atom, and the Manga/Anime Revolution

Professor Risley and the Imperial Japanese Troupe: How an American Acrobat Introduced Circus to Japan—and Japan to the West

SELECT TRANSLATIONS

Mobile Suit Gundam: Awakening, Escalation, Confrontation, by Yoshiyuki Tomino

Gaku Stories, by Makoto Shiina (U.S. title: *My Boy: A Father's Memories*)

Jack and Betty Stories, by Yoshinori Shimizu

The Four Immigrants Manga: A Japanese Experience in San Francisco, 1904–1924, by Henry Yoshitaka Kiyama

Starting Point: 1979–1996, by Hayao Miyazaki (translated with Beth Cary)

Turning Point: 1997–2002, by Hayao Miyazaki (translated with Beth Cary)

The Osamu Tezuka Story: A Life in Manga and Anime, by Toshio Ban and Tezuka Productions

My Heart Sutra

A WORLD IN 260 CHARACTERS

Frederik L. Schodt

Stone Bridge Press • Berkeley, California

Published by
Stone Bridge Press
P. O. Box 8208, Berkeley, CA 94707
TEL 510-524-8732 • sbp@stonebridge.com • www.stonebridge.com

Printed in the United States of America.

10 9 8 7 6 5 4 3 2 1   2023 2022 2021 2020

p-ISBN 978-1-61172-062-4
e-ISBN 978-1-61172-944-3

This book is dedicated

to little Mason and Jacob, who kept supplying smiles and laughter, and often asked me to "do that *shiki-shiki* chant thing."

Contents

Foreword

This is a book of essays about the Heart Sutra, or the "Heart of the Perfection of Wisdom Sutra," also known in Sanskrit as the *Prajñāpāramitā Hṛdaya Sūtra*. It is one of the shortest Buddhist texts and one of most popular in East Asia (and increasingly the world), chanted, copied, and contemplated by millions. It can be described in many ways—puzzling, profound, convoluted, crazy, radical, revolutionary, mysterious, magical, a gateway to Mahayana Buddhism, and an entirely new way of viewing the universe. With phrases such as "form is not different from emptiness" and "no form, no sensation, no perception, no formation, no consciousness; no eyes, no ears, no nose, no tongue, no body, no mind ...," much of it at first seems a tangled mass of negatives and double negatives, all of which could be read as a long disclaimer before the great "reveal" of a mantra at the end.

In the same spirit, I feel obliged to give readers a few disclaimers, about what this book is, and is not.

- This book is, in a sense, an inversion of the hundreds of existing books about the Heart Sutra, for I do not personally try to "explain" the sutra's true meaning to readers. The reason? It would be presumptuous of me, because I see studying and trying to understand it as my own daily, if not lifelong task. There are many fine books in English by courageous experts who concentrate on explanations, including those by D. T. Suzuki and Edward Conze and, more recently, by Red Pine, the 14th Dalai Lama, Donald S. Lopez Jr., Thich Nhat Hanh, and Kazuaki Tanahashi, to name only a few. As the title of my book hints, this is about *my* Heart Sutra and my fascination with it and how it is used.

• Unlike most authors on the Heart Sutra, I am not connected to a religion or a religious sect, and I am not an academic. I began this book with purely personal motives, not even sure it would yield anything worth publishing, for to me it was a challenge—a way to sort my own thoughts and experiences and satisfy my own curiosity. I have had an abiding obsession with the sutra and wanted to learn why, so at times it is also an archaeology of my own memory. And I wanted to look at the Heart Sutra as an unusual social and religious phenomenon. In the process, something designed to be short became longer. But like the Heart Sutra itself, it is still relatively succinct.

• Unlike many writers on the Heart Sutra, who often provide their own brand-new translations, in this book I do not. Instead, I encourage readers to find translations they like among the fine ones that already exist. For reference I have included a copy of Xuanzang's Chinese version, along with a traditional Sōtō Zen English version, and a translation from the Centre of Buddhist Studies at the University of Hong Kong. Some readers may nonetheless wonder why

I pay so much attention in this book to language, to the way it is used, and to translation in general. The short answer is that I have a long career in interpreting and translating and an abiding interest in cross-cultural communications, which the Heart Sutra also symbolizes.

• There is little discussion in this book about Tibet or Korea or Vietnam or Mongolia or other countries where the Heart Sutra is also used. Instead, I have concentrated mainly on Greater China and Japan, or what might be called the "Sino-Japanese character zone." Some readers may wonder why, and it is because an orthographically identical version of the sutra has been in use in this region for at least 1,400 years. It is the "translation" attributed to the Chinese monk Xuanzang, arguably the "master version," and nearly all other language translations, including those in English, stem from it. Another reason is that I have some language skills that help in this area, especially Japanese. In both Korea and Vietnam, traditional ideograms have unfortunately (in my opinion) fallen out of use among the general public, often by government fiat that cuts people off from their own cultural roots. But even more to the point, I have no expertise in classical Sanskrit, Tibetan, Korean, Mongolian, or Vietnamese, and I shall not pretend otherwise.

This leaves lots of room for criticism, which is always welcome, but I hope that some readers will enjoy taking this journey with me, as I zig and zag like a butterfly through sometimes strange territories and subjects on a quirky quest, alighting here and there to listen to what others have to say, and to observe more closely. In the process, who knows? Together, we might discover something new and interesting, as well as useful, even taste some nectar!

Before jumping in, some minor housekeeping is in order. Rendering Asian names in English often makes authors want to tear their hair out in frustration (at least what little is left after writing books). The first problem with Chinese and Japanese names is their order. In this case, I have tried to maintain native Chinese/Japanese order of "last name" first, "first name" last, making an exception for people who have established themselves in the West. For example, for the calligrapher-author Kazuaki Tanahashi, who lives in Berkeley, California, and goes by "Kaz," I use American name order because that is what he uses.

Romanizing Chinese names also runs into the problem of different systems used in different eras. For example, most books written about China in the twentieth century used a system called Wade-Giles. Now, most use the pinyin system. Thus, the name of the most famous Heart Sutra translator/compiler/popularizer was once usually known as Hsüan-tsang. Today he is known in pinyin as Xuanzang. When quoting older English-language texts, I have kept the Wade-Giles renderings used by the original authors, but for newer texts I have used renderings in pinyin, if that is what the authors used. Turning everything into a knotted mass of complications is the fact that many Chinese people have more than one name, and many overseas or Hong Kong Chinese have used Wade-Giles or other systems of romanization for their names for generations, so it would not be proper to change them to pinyin. I hope readers will understand and show the author some mercy.

Finally, foreign words and names that have sunk deep into

the English language need no diacritical marks or macrons, so I have left them as is. *Sūtra*, therefore, is written as "sutra," unless I am quoting someone else's usage. *Kyōto* is Kyoto. *Tōkyō* is Tokyo. And for Chinese, I have followed the *Chicago Manual of Style* recommendation and left off tonal marks for modern pinyin, except when there is specific value in including them. For visual reference, I have also occasionally used terms with Chinese or Japanese ideograms as is.

Every writer needs help, and I have been shown a great deal of kindness by many people. I am especially indebted to the following people: to the lovely Fiammetta Hsu, my wife, who has patiently listened to me talk about the Heart Sutra for what seems like an eternity and accompanied me on travels to odd places and helped photograph them and provide a link to greater China; to Mark Blum, Buddhist Studies Professor at the University of California, Berkeley, who checked a particularly difficult chapter and agreed to being incessantly badgered with esoteric questions, despite his busy schedule; to John Nelson, Professor of East Asian Religions at the University of San Francisco, for bravely volunteering to be a reader, giving stellar advice, and during a pandemic low point leading me backpacking in the Sierras; to Leonard Rifas, who I believe has read drafts of every book I have written and always, always provided on-target recommendations; to David Olson, for his insights, meticulous mind, and push toward clarity; and to my dear friend and dharma-hero, the monk-priest Daigaku Rummé, who has helped me continually on this project and other adventures in my life, including officiating at my wedding in 2006 where the Heart Sutra was read. And I would be negligent if I did not thank Peter Goodman, my publisher and editor and old friend, who continually consents to publish my overly niche books; Linda Ronan, for always wonderful cover designs; John Sockolov, for help indexing; and Michael Palmer, who works valiantly to publicize my odd books in an increasingly tough publishing world.

For interviews and advice and special assistance, I also want to credit the following people. To avoid the nightmarish problems that occur with mixing nationalities, last names are listed first, and first names are listed last.

Applebaum, Ted | Attwood, Jayarava (for all his years of hard work) | Carey, Bill | Chen, Beverly | Ciner-Schodt family | Clements, Jonathan | Cook, Jared | Degelman family | Dijs, Frederik | Ejiri, Emi | Foster, Matthew | Gleason, Alan | Green, Frederik | Hayama, Judy | Honda, Dōryū | Hsu, Yinchiu | Inoue, Nanae | Ishiguro, Hiroshi | Ishimatsu, Hisayuki | Isobe, Yumi | Kaneko, Miwa | Katō, Kazumitsu | Katz, Milton | Kelly, Larry | Kirchner, Thomas (Yūhō) | Kiyama family | Koren, Leonard | Kotoku, Minoru | Kotyk, Jeffrey | Kudō, Noriyuki | Larrett, Raymond | Larson, Gerald J. | Law family | McBride, Brennan | Masters, Pat | Mikami, Kōraku | Mimatsu, Kanpō | Mori, Masahiro | Nattier, Jan | Ogawa, Kōhei | Ogawa, Mayumi | Porter, Bill (Red Pine) | Rudolph, Deborah | Sekikawa, Natsuo | Shiu, Henry | Snyder, Gary | So, Brenda | Sullivan family (Anisia, Jacob, Mason, Mikey) | Takagi family | Tanahashi, Kazuaki | Tokioka, Keiko & Satoko | Twine family | Van Nest family | Watanabe, Shōgo | Xiong, Shanjun. And special thanks to the two Good Samaritans (one Twinkle Sales and one unknown) who helped me during a motorcycle crash on November 12, 2019, as I was finishing a draft of this manuscript.

般若波羅蜜多心經　　　　唐三藏法師玄奘譯

觀自在菩薩。行深般若波羅蜜多時。照見五蘊皆空。度一切苦厄。舍利子。色不異空。空不異色。色即是空。空即是色。受想行識亦復如是。舍利子。是諸法空相。不生不滅。不垢不淨不增不減。是故空中。無色。無受想行識。無眼耳鼻舌身意。無色聲香味觸法。無眼界。乃至無意識界。無無明。亦無無明盡。乃至無老死。亦無老死盡。無苦集滅道。無智亦無得。以無所得故。菩提薩埵。依般若波羅蜜多故。心無罣礙。無罣礙故。無有恐怖。遠離顛倒夢想。究竟涅槃。三世諸佛。依般若波羅蜜多故。得阿耨多羅三藐三菩提。故知般若波羅蜜多。是大神咒。是大明咒是無上咒。是無等等咒。能除一切苦。眞實不虛故。說般若波羅蜜多咒即說咒曰

揭帝揭帝　般羅揭帝　般羅僧揭帝菩提僧莎訶

般若波羅蜜多心經

Base Chinese version of the Heart Sutra included in the *Taishō shinshū daizōkyō* (the Buddhist Tripiṭaka), vol. 8 T251, noted as having been "Translated by Tang Tripiṭaka Master Xuanzang." The main body of the text has 260 characters, as is still the case in China.

Heart of Great Perfect Wisdom Sutra

Avalokiteshvara Bodhisattva, when deeply practicing Prajna Paramita, clearly saw that all five aggregates are empty and thus relieved all suffering. Shariputra, form does not differ from emptiness, emptiness does not differ from form. Form itself is emptiness, emptiness itself form. Sensations, perceptions, formations, and consciousness are also like this. Shariputra, all dharmas are marked by emptiness. They neither arise nor cease, are neither defiled nor pure, neither increase nor decrease. Therefore, given emptiness, there is no form, no sensation, no perception, no formation, no consciousness; no eyes, no ears, no nose, no tongue, no body, no mind, no sight, no sound, no smell, no taste, no touch, no object of mind, no realm of sight ... no realm of mind consciousness. There is neither ignorance nor extinction of ignorance, neither old age and death, nor extinction of old age and death. No suffering, no cause, no cessation, no path, no knowledge, and no attainment. With nothing to attain, a Bodhisattva relies on Prajna Paramita, and thus the mind is without hindrance. Without hindrance, there is no fear. Far beyond all inverted views, one realizes Nirvana. All Buddhas of past, present, and future rely on Prajna Paramita and thereby attain unsurpassed, complete, perfect enlightenment. Therefore know the Prajna Paramita as the great miraculous mantra, the great bright mantra, the supreme mantra, the incomparable mantra, which removes all suffering and is true, not false. Therefore we proclaim the Prajna Paramita mantra, the mantra that says: "Gaté Gaté Paragaté Parasamgaté Bodhi Svaha!"

Available at https://global.sotozen-net.or.jp/eng/practice/sutra/pdf/01/04.pdf.

A DESCRIPTION OF THE HEART SUTRA

The Heart Sutra articulates the doctrine of "emptiness." But this "emptiness" must not be understood as the denial of phenomenal existence—it is not nihilism. What it teaches is that everything is dependently arisen from conditions; an event (a "thing") occurs if and only if the adequacy of conditions obtains. Since everything is dependently arisen, there is no such thing as an eternally abiding entity. The doctrine of emptiness also spells out the relativity of all views. When one acquires this Wisdom of "emptiness," one will realize that all physical and mental events are in a constant process of change, and accordingly everything can be changed by modifying the conditions. Understanding the relativity of all standpoints will also prevent one from becoming irrationally attached to things. In this way, one will come to be free from mental obstructions, and attain to perfect harmony and bliss. At the same time, with the understanding that all are dependently arisen, one will treasure and make good use of the conditions that are available, realizing the idea of benefiting oneself and others.

Displayed on a bronze plaque at the bottom of the Wisdom Trail on Lantau Island, Hong Kong.

1

My Mantra

On September 12, 2016, I was scheduled to go to Los Angeles to work as an interpreter at a conference. The job was to be held in the Japanese American National Museum and focus on aspects of modern Japanese culture. I had a reservation on Southwest Airlines Flight 1518, scheduled to leave Oakland, California, at 7:25 am and arriving in Burbank airport. It was a regular flight for many businesspeople going to Los Angeles, a short hop of about 325 miles, or a little over an hour. I fly a lot and wasn't worried about the trip. I was mainly worried about my job, since it was to be simultaneous interpreting of a wide-ranging subject area, packed with unfamiliar jargon requiring advance memorization. I worried that I might not be able to keep up with fast speakers in both languages. And as usual in the interpreting business, I just hoped my interpreting partner and I would get through the job successfully, without any complaints, and then happily head home the same day.

On a clear day, the flight from Oakland down to Burbank and the LA area affords spectacular views of California. Out the right windows of the plane there are beaches and the vast

Pacific Ocean; directly below, the low-lying coastal mountain range runs north and south; out the left windows, the broad plains of the fertile San Joaquin Valley stretch way out toward the distant, soaring, and sometimes still-snow-capped Sierra Nevada range. But on the 12th, about halfway into the flight, not far from the city of San Luis Obispo, the captain came on the loudspeaker and suddenly announced that the plane had developed a problem with one of the engines, that we didn't have enough "thrust" and would have to turn back to Oakland. It was a calm announcement, and the passengers—many of whom presumably took the flight nearly every morning—all seemed to take it quite calmly. But it made me feel a bit anxious, if for no other reason than the fact that our airplane, a Boeing 737, had only two engines.

RELIGION AND ME

I grew up overseas, and because my parents were members of the Foreign Service, airplane travel was always part of my life. It has remained so, but I've never particularly enjoyed flying. As a tiny boy, in the days of propeller planes, when there was far more noise, turbulence, and problems with cabin pressurization, on take-offs and landings I would sometimes clutch a tiny New Testament—the "pocket" sort often handed out for free to children at Sunday School in the mid-1950s—and try to recite the Lord's Prayer in hopes that the plane would not crash. That Testament is still on a shelf, with my nickname "Fred" scrawled in the shaky, primitive pencil letters of a very small boy.

I was raised a Christian, but I've drifted from that world. My somewhat religious father went to church when he could,

Buddha in the Redwoods.

accompanied by my dutiful mother who, except for enjoying choir singing, was usually happy to stay away and perhaps an atheist at heart. My brother and I were baptized in a Presbyterian church in Washington, D.C., and attended a Lutheran church in Norway and occasionally a Methodist church in Australia. Mainly, I remember the pent-up energy that resulted from being imprisoned in narrow pews and four walls for an hour, and the knock-down fights with my brother that often later ensued. Sometimes, in Sunday schools, we were given religious paraphernalia. As a child, on my bedroom wall, I had a wooden plaque, rounded and spoked in the shape of a ship's wheel, showing a profoundly hippy-looking Jesus calmly navigating storms (presumably of life). It always gave me solace. I also had a plastic cross that glowed in the dark; in retrospect, given the era, it may have been somewhat radioactive, much like early watch dials, but under the covers at night when feeling insecure it, too, seemed to calm me. On my deathbed I'll probably see images of Jesus, long ago burned into my brain cells, flicker past me.

When I was thirteen, in Australia, my father gave me the choice of continuing to attend church or taking my dog—an unrepentant Welsh corgi—to dog-training school; of course, I chose the latter. When I was seventeen, at an international high school in Tokyo, Japan, my parents were given another diplomatic assignment, but I chose to remain in Japan to graduate. I lived in a tiny dormitory mainly for missionary children (which I was not), and on Sunday we were usually required to attend some sort of Christian service. I often attended local Quaker meetings, which were almost Zen-like in their minimalism and probably the closest modern Christianity gets to

Buddhism. I was a bit out of sync with at least one of my dorm mates, who viewed me as nearly beyond redemption, later writing in my senior yearbook, "I would challenge you to read the New Testament.... Some people may call me a religious fanatic, but if I have tasted honey and you have not, I am not going to shut up."

In the fall of 1967 something happened that affected me. I say "something," because memory is tricky. In my mind, a famous American evangelist was speaking at my school's small gym, telling us that if we didn't take Jesus Christ as our savior we would go to Hell instead of Heaven. Given that Japan has a vanishingly small Christian population of only around 1% and given that I had grown up in a highly multicultural world, this message, rather than bold and courageous, seemed terribly misguided and wrong. All those Japanese—whose culture I admired—were they condemned to suffer in hell for eternity, and me with them? I even remember the evangelist as the late, legendary Billy Graham, who visited Tokyo that year on what he called a "Crusade," speaking in front of an adoring crowd of thousands in Tokyo's Budōkan stadium. Yet there is no record in the school archives of him ever visiting the school. Some of my more religious dorm mates did indeed go downtown to hear him, but no one seems to remember him coming out to our school. Is my memory assembled from their reports? Is it a phantom, or conflated with some other event or other speaker at the time? Real or imagined, to me it has always been real, and troubling. In a sense, something turned a switch in my mind.

After that, my contact with official Christianity more or less ended. I still have deep appreciation for its emphasis on love and compassion and forgiveness. I believe the world would be a shallow place without any of the Abrahamic or monotheistic religions. But I am not comfortable with the intolerance and cruelty to which the "mono" in "monotheism" can so easily lead. Nor am I comfortable with the always anthropocentric—or human-centric—structure of most religions.

I now consider myself religious only in a vague way—made up of something like a religious and philosophical soup, I might say, starting with a vague base of Christianity to which has been added animism, nature worship, transcendentalism, the Gaia theory, Buddhism, a dash of Taoism, and other poorly understood systems. Neither atheist, nor agnostic, I'm probably pantheistic, for I'm willing to believe in multiple "higher authorities," but I have no formal affiliation with any specific organized religion. Nor do I have the discipline to completely immerse myself in one, for to me most seem based on a few profound insights, wrapped in layers of complexity and dogma, infused with the usual human arrogance and delusion. While Buddhism has always appealed to me on an intellectual level, I must confess that I am not even a practicing Buddhist, or even a meditator. In short, I'm a typically modern, lazy, only occasionally spiritual being. And after watching too many people drift into Christian fundamentalism, or later into various Asian religious cults, or even into political extremes, I've developed an allergy to any sort of blind faith. When I look at animals and trees and the sky I will never be convinced that any human knows all the answers.

Having said all that, I'm not immune to a certain envy of those who have what might be called "faith." And the closest I come to this religious "faith" is a fascination with and fetish for the Heart Sutra, or what is known in Sanskrit as the *Prajñā-pāramitā Hṛdaya Sūtra*, sometimes translated as "Heart of the Perfection of Wisdom Sutra." Other religions may have prayers or scriptures somehow similar in usage or philosophy. That, I do not know. This book is about the sutra that I found, about my relationship to it, and my explorations into its usage, both ancient and modern.

A RESOLUTION

When the captain of my plane first made his announcement, I felt in control of my anxiety. But something seemed odd. Why should we turn back to Oakland because we didn't have enough thrust in an engine if we were half-way to Burbank? Wouldn't it make more sense to go on to Burbank? My doubts amplified, and then we circled in the sky once, twice—in my memory three times.

On the third time, I felt a true surge of anxiety. It was September 12, after all, only a day after the anniversary of the notorious terrorist attack on New York by hijacked planes back in 2001. And while most people might not have made the same association, for me, odd as it may seem, the circling in the sky made me think of Japan Airlines Flight 123, one of the worst disasters in airline history. On August 12, 1985, the four-engine 747 jumbo had been on a regularly scheduled flight from Tokyo to Osaka. A bulkhead and subsequent hydraulic failure caused the pilots to lose directional control, and after weaving and circling crazily in the sky for an appalling thirty minutes the plane smashed into the mountains outside of Tokyo. Of the 524 passengers, all died except 4, who were grievously injured. Many had been returning to their family homes to celebrate

Obon, the All-Souls Festival of Japan, when the souls of ancestors are said to return to their homeland.[1]

The accident created a wound in the Japanese national psyche, and in trying to absorb it people would later write books, create mournful songs, movies, and even a manga, or comic book, about it. In what to me was always one of the most disturbing ideas at the time, passengers had had over thirty minutes to contemplate their doom, and several even wrote out farewell notes that were later found. Among the notables on the plane was Sakamoto Kyū, the singer who had popularized one of my favorite songs, "Ue wo muite" ("I Look Up as I Walk"), an extraordinarily mournful ballad. When exported to the United States in 1963 it had been given the improbable name of "Sukiyaki" (presumably because that was one of the few Japanese words Americans then knew) and become the first and only Japanese song to top the U.S. pop charts.

So, while staring out the window of my far more modern plane, while others seemed to take it all in stride, I had my white-knuckle moments, with too much time for contemplation added. In such situations, I've always struggled to put things into perspective, no matter how hard it might be to do so. We're all going to die at some point, right, so why worry? After all, one of the tricks I have used as a child (and even as an adult) on boarding airplanes has been to assume that I'm already dead. It helps, but it's not enough. Under extreme strain, the mind hopes for some sort of prayer, some sort of incantation, something simply to cling to psychologically. When actually dying on the battlefield, soldiers are often said to call for their mothers; but I wasn't at that stage yet, since the plane hadn't crashed, or even really lost control.

What I needed was just to steel myself. As a child, I might have recited the Lord's Prayer with absolutely no comprehension of what I was saying, but I no longer remembered it. At that moment on September 12, 2016, had I had the presence of mind, I would have recited the entire Heart Sutra. It's one of the shortest of all Buddhist sutras, and it fit perfectly with my view of the world at that moment. The only problem was that, while holding out myself as something of a devotee of the Heart Sutra, out of sheer intellectual lethargy I had never memorized the entire thing.

What I did know very well was the mantra at the end of the sutra. The part that goes, *Gaté gaté pāragaté pārasaṃgaté bodhi svāhā* (*gaté* is pronounced more like "ghateh"). It's only six words long in transcribed Sanskrit and only 18 ideograms in Chinese and Japanese out of a total of 260 (or 262, if you are from Japan). It has a nice melodic ring to it, and for decades now it has always been my secret weapon, my personal incantation for salvation against pain and fear and mental turmoil.

After circling three times, the captain turned the plane north and, with presumably limited thrust in one engine, we limped back to Oakland Airport. We landed safely, and Southwest Airlines, to their credit, with extraordinary speed and efficiency transferred all the passengers—who seemed to take it all in stride—to another, mechanically uncompromised plane. We took off once more on the hour-long flight to Burbank, and to my surprise I even made it in time for my interpreting assignment in Los Angeles. The company also gave all its inconvenienced passengers a $150 voucher for future flights. I hadn't expected much, and merely felt relieved, so I was entirely happy. Much later, however, the incident would cause me to spend many hours exploring the dusty corners of my brain, trying to understand how I first became enamored of the Heart Sutra mantra, and how I had even learned of it in the first place. This made me want to know more. Eventually, I realized that contemplating the Heart Sutra, memorizing it, chanting it, copying it, even writing about it, could be my practice, my fragile toehold in what most people might think of as the world of faith.

2

How I Met the Mantra

To the best of my memory I first heard the Heart Sutra mantra being recited in 1974 when I attended a poetry reading by Allen Ginsberg in Los Angeles. Why this should have been the first time is a bit of a mystery. I had even read a translation of the entire sutra two years previously, but it was the sound of the mantra that day that resonated in my mind.

There are few countries in the world where the Heart Sutra has become so woven into daily life as Japan. I lived there three times: in high school from 1965 to '68, as a college student from 1970 to '72. and finally from 1975 to '78 as a postgraduate student and professional translator. Yet I have no memory of ever hearing or seeing anything related to the Heart Sutra the first two times. It is a classic example, I suspect, of the truism that the eyes cannot see, the ears cannot hear, and the mind cannot understand unless ready to do so. When I lived in Japan during high school I traveled several times around the main island on my old motorcycle and visited many temples, often collecting stamped calligraphic records of my visits and sometimes (with my roommate of the time) even staying overnight at them. Yet in those days I could not speak or read Japanese, so even if I had been surrounded by the Heart Sutra I would not have seen it; even if I had heard monks chanting it I would not have known it. The second time I lived in Japan, attending a Japanese university, I could read and speak Japanese, but my interests lay elsewhere. I was, again, not ready.

In a personal journal from 1974 I recently discovered the ticket I had pasted in for Ginsberg's LA poetry reading, where I first heard, or recognized hearing, the mantra. The ticket shows that he appeared with the yogi-guru Bhagavan Das on May 10, 1974, at the old Embassy Auditorium on 843 South Grand Avenue.

I was twenty-four then, living in Los Angeles and working for a Japanese company as a tour guide and tour escort, taking tourists not only around sights in Los Angeles but sometimes as far away as Mexico and Canada. It was a fairly short job, lasting only about a year and a half, a comma in a larger coming-of-age paragraph. Before and after that I had been in Santa Barbara for a few years in a household of close friends, living an unanchored life doing odd jobs, taking multiple hitchhiking trips around America, and occasionally writing undeniably bad poetry. Perhaps because I had long lived overseas and in Japan, I for some time had had wild fantasies of walking around America writing haiku. Although a member of the "hippy" generation, at least in terms of age, I identified more with the older Beatniks who (to me at least) seemed to read and think and write more and even—discounting their often prodigious consumptions of alcohol and cigarettes—do fewer drugs. For me, it was period of learning about not only my confused "self" but my own country, about which I frankly knew little. And for me, and many others in my milieu, the Beat poets such as

The ticket.

Jack Kerouac, Gary Snyder, and Allen Ginsberg formed a pantheon of heroes. I especially admired the way they often found beauty in the ordinary, and even in the downtrodden and dispossessed in American society. But I can't say that I was a deep follower of any Beat poet in particular.

After attending the Ginsberg reading in LA I scrawled the mantra in my journal. As if to signal how important it seemed, shortly later I somehow incorporated it into the chorus of an amateurish rambling song I wrote, blending in references to the star-formation Pleiades and the Heart Sutra mantra. In the mountains behind Santa Barbara I sometimes also enjoyed chanting the mantra in the evening with friends as the red sun sank out of sight into the Pacific. Thereafter, references to it started to appear in my journal with increasing frequency.

Early in 1975, after Nixon's impeachment and near the end of the Vietnam War, after hitchhiking across country, there is an entry about circumambulating the White House with a pal and, in an act of Dada-esque youthful exuberance, chanting the Heart Sutra mantra in an attempt to exorcise it.

Of Ginsberg I knew little, except that he was a poet of considerable and complex genius in the tradition of the mid-nineteenth century Walt Whitman, highly eccentric and fearlessly honest about his own human and often deep flaws. Nearly seventeen years later, I would be briefly married to a Japanese woman whose college senior thesis had been "Zen Influence in American Literature." She would later turn to fine arts photography and essays (before becoming a teacher of ancient hula in Tokyo) and photograph several legendary Beatniks. It was a failed marriage but through her I at least got to meet Ginsberg and understand his milieu far better.

Ginsberg was arguably at the peak of his public fame in 1974. He was forty-eight years old, and it had already been eighteen years since publication of his most famous poem— "Howl," a visceral condemnation of 1950s conformity and materialism—which had scandalized conservative America. At the reading I attended in 1974, Ginsberg largely refrained from the homoerotic material that he often delighted in using as a sort of shock-therapy. Instead, he read mainly from a long, beautiful poem of a far more spiritual bent, called "Mind Breaths." It described him meditating at a Tibetan Buddhist guru's retreat in the Tetons, his exhaled breath traveling all around the world. At some point, while playing his beloved rectangular box harmonium (that always emitted a narcotic droning sound) he chanted the Heart Sutra. Whether he chanted the whole sutra or not, I don't know. It is the mantra portion that I remember, which takes up only a small portion of its entirety.

Ginsberg was speaking then on what was sometimes referred to as the "hippy circuit." It was the tail end of a boom, almost a rush hour, in religious gurus in America. It had not only brought a long string of charismatic figures from the exotic East but also created a space for adventurous Americans to go there to study and then return (perhaps overconfidently, with new Indian names) to impart a new type of knowledge to their compatriots. Oddly, I have no memory at all of the other speaker at the event—Bhagavan Das (né Kermit Michael Riggs). Also puzzling is how I wound up going and even got there, since it was quite a ways from where I lived at the time in sprawling Los Angeles, I have never owned a car, and it was the sort of thing I would never have gone to on my own.

Today I marvel at Ginsberg's connection to the Heart Sutra and especially its mantra. He was eclectic, almost promiscuous, in his religiosity; like many Beat Generation poets, he was attracted to a variety of Eastern religions in a quest for a different view of reality. While described as a practicing Buddhist, he crossed many sectarian lines, dabbling in Japanese and Chinese Mahayana thought, ultimately settling (mainly) on Tibetan or Tantric/esoteric Buddhism. But Ginsberg dabbled in Jewish mysticism and Hinduism as well, often incorporating Hindu chants into his poetry readings and performances, reading OM and Hare Krishna mantras.

Nearly every thought has a lineage. In 1974, the Heart Sutra was still relatively unknown in the West, but Ginsberg had already been chanting it—and especially the mantra—for many years. He had become fascinated by Buddhism in the early 1950s, when he read Daisetsu Teitarō ("D. T.") Suzuki's books, *An Introduction to Zen Buddhism* and its companion, *Manual of Zen Buddhism* (first published in 1934 and 1935, respectively). The latter volume had a full translation of the Heart Sutra.[2]

Perhaps even more than these books, Ginsberg's early interest in Buddhism was amplified by his friendship with the writer Jack Kerouac and especially the poet Gary Snyder.

Kerouac, better known as a Catholic, became famous for his jazz-infused best-selling novels such as *On the Road*, but at the beginning of the 1950s he was also a serious student of Buddhism, particularly the Diamond Sutra. His writings on it and about Buddhism in general would later be published as a 420-page book under the title *Some of the Dharma*, written between 1953 and 1956. He, too, also read early books containing translations of the Heart Sutra, such as D. T. Suzuki's works and Dwight Goddard's 1932 *The Buddhist Bible.*[3] Not coincidentally, the co-protagonist of his other best-selling 1958 novel, *The Dharma Bums*, was a Buddhism-infused character named Japhy Ryder, based on the real character of Kerouac and Ginsberg's mutual friend, the poet Gary Snyder.

Snyder's fascination with Buddhism had started even earlier, also from reading works by D. T. Suzuki. As Snyder recalls it, in 1951 he had been hitchhiking from the West Coast to Indiana:

> In the middle of Nevada, on old Interstate 40, there was a period of about five hours where nobody would give me a ride. As I stood there in the middle of the

sagebrush flats, I was reading through a chapter
of Suzuki's *Essays in Zen Buddhism*, First Series, and
I hit on some phrases that turned my mind totally
around.[4]

Suzuki's *Essays* made no mention of the Heart Sutra specifically, but Snyder also read his 1935 *Manual of Zen Buddhism*,
a book that did contain a translation, and he began to pursue
Buddhism even more seriously. Between 1953 and 1955 he
studied Chinese and Japanese at the Department of East Asian
Languages in Berkeley, California, and while there he met both
Kerouac and Ginsberg. In 1956 he went to Japan for the first
of several sojourns, formally studying Zen in Kyoto at what
was called the "First Zen Institute of America in Japan," on the
grounds of the famous Rinzai sect temple Daitoku-ji and also
at nearby Shōkoku-ji temple, under Zen abbot Miura Isshū.
As part of his studies he was required by Miura to memorize
the Heart Sutra, and chanting became an integral part of his
life, part of his daily practice—so much so that back in California much later, in 1973, a poem titled "One Should Not Talk
to a Skilled Hunter about What Is Forbidden by the Buddha"
reveals that he was still in the habit of chanting it when, for
example, skinning a road-kill fox for its pelt.[5] Yet even for
Snyder, when he started studying in Japan, understanding
the sutra intellectually was difficult. According to a friend in
America, Alex Wayman, Snyder wrote asking if he could find
out what it meant, complaining that he couldn't find anyone
around him in Japan who could explain it to him.[6]

Intellectual comprehension aside, the Heart Sutra has
often had a practical, talismanic component for those who have

memorized it, and this aspect of it soon came in handy for Snyder. Early on, he fell in with some *yamabushi*, or shamanistic mountain ascetics in Japan. These positively medieval-looking nature worshipers carry metal staves and conch shells and wear straw sandals and sometimes a hemp cloth over-robe with the Heart Sutra written on it. They follow a mixture of esoteric or tantric Buddhism mixed with Shinto, the native animistic religion of Japan. As Snyder described his initiation much later,

> They said, "O.K., we're going to see if you are one of us." They told me to climb up a five-hundred-foot vertical rock pitch while chanting the Heart Sutra. Luckily, I knew the Heart Sutra, so that was O.K. Then they said, "Now we're going to initiate you." They tied a rope around my ankles and hung me over a cliff and said, "We'll drop you if you don't tell the truth," and they started asking me questions.[7]

Snyder soon also set a direct example for Allen Ginsberg on how to incorporate the Heart Sutra into his life. In an expansive interview much later, titled "The Vomit of a Mad Tyger," Ginsberg mentions going on a pilgrimage to India in 1962 where he joined up with Snyder and Snyder's then-wife, Joan Kyger, who had come from Kyoto.

> In a cave at Ellora, Gary sat himself down and chanted the Prajnaparamita Sutra in Sino-Japanese, with echoes of the cave around, and that blew my mind. It was such an extended, long, and obviously

spiritual breath, vocalized, that I got really interested
and asked him about what it meant, and why he was
doing it in Japanese, and what was the history of it.[8]

"Prajnaparamita Sutra" was Ginsberg's way of referring to
the very short Heart Sutra, or the *Prajñāpāramitā Hṛdaya Sūtra*,
which is only one sutra in a larger body of Prajñāpāramitā
texts, many of which are of such a length that no one would
actually chant them. And what he refers to as "Sino-Japanese"
is really Snyder's Japanese pronunciation of a Chinese translation or compilation. Ginsberg had obviously seen or read
the sutra before in translation in English texts, but his choice
of words seems to indicate that he had at least never heard it
chanted. In a different translated English version, this sutra
and especially its mantra would thereafter become one of
Ginsberg's favorite chants, done in all sorts of public forums,
including demonstrations and poetry readings, often accompanied with his harmonium or at the minimum his equally
beloved finger-cymbals.

In the same article, Ginsberg mentions a 1972
Buddhist-themed poetry retreat in Boulder, Colorado, where
he again read the "Prajnaparamita Sutra" with Gary Sny-
der, the "desert rat-Japanese-Zen-lunatic poet-meditator"
Sakaki Nanao, and Ginsberg's Tibetan guru-teacher Chogyam
Trungpa.

I was going to do some singing GATE GATE, and we
each chanted our own version of Prajnaparamita:
Gary, the regular Japanese, "Kanji Zai Bo Satsu Gyo-
gin Han Nya Ha Ra Mi Ta Ji ..." and then Nanao a

long KAAANNJJII using an extended breath, a beautiful hollow voice, and Trungpa Rinpoche almost in
pedestrian offhand Tibetan. I did a version that I had
worked out from Suzuki Roshi's English telegraphese
translation.[9]

In this case, "singing GATE GATE" (*gaté gaté*) refers to
the Heart Sutra mantra, sometimes romanized from Japanese as *gyatei gyatei*. The "Suzuki" to which Ginsberg refers
is not the Rinzai Zen sect's Daisetsu Teitarō Suzuki, author
of the early books containing a popular translation of the
Heart Sutra, but Shunryū Suzuki, the Sōtō Zen–sect priest
who came to America in 1959, served as the first head of the
San Francisco Zen Center, and greatly helped propagate Zen
among late-twentieth-century Americans. In Shunryū Suzuki's
translation of the Heart Sutra, rendered in rather charming
and somewhat broken English—or what Ginsberg calls "telegraphese"—the first line of the sutra began with "*Avalokitesvara
Bodhisattva practice deep prajna paramita when ...*" The mantra
itself was also translated into English as "Gone, gone, to the
other shore gone, reach (go) enlightenment-accomplish."
Ginsberg had met Shunryū Suzuki after returning from his trip
to India, and in the mid- to late sixties had received permission
to use and later adapt this translation (with the help of the
Tibetan llama Gelek Rinpoche) to his own lyrical, poetic style.
Thereafter he would sing/chant it widely in public at poetry
readings and also political demonstrations (slightly off-key
and with a self-deprecating sense of humor), but he usually
sang the short mantra, or what he calls the "GATE GATE" portion, in its original Sanskrit transliteration, following it with

揭帝揭帝

波羅揭帝

波羅僧揭帝

菩提僧莎訶

"Gaté gaté pāragaté pārasaṃgaté bodhi svāhā!" The mantra in its most popular rendition, in Sino-Japanese (read right to left, vertically). In the earliest surviving renditions (see pp. 15 and p. 136), the character 般 was often used instead of 波 to approximate the Sanskrit sound of "pa."

his very loose English interpretation: "*All gone, all gone, all over gone, all gone sky high now old mind soul, ah ...*" And this is presumably similar to what he would have done in Los Angeles on May 10, 1974, when I first remember hearing the mantra.[10]

Ever the performer, years later, in 1982, Ginsberg would also collaborate with the punk rock group The Clash on their CD of that year, *Combat Rock*. At the end on a track called "Ghetto Defendant," where he provided a droning background denunciation of the evils of ideology and repression, he can be heard chanting this same version of the Heart Sutra mantra.[11]

LISTENING TO THE MANTRA

In today's world, without leaving the safety of your armchair, you can listen to monks around the world hypnotically chanting the Heart Sutra. On YouTube, you can listen to it in various European languages and in Asian languages such as Tibetan, Nepali, Indian, Korean, Vietnamese, Japanese, and both Cantonese and Mandarin Chinese. Sometimes, if the words in the translation have a nice meter to them, the sutra is also shown performed as music by popular singers. Given the linguistic and cultural barriers and the millennia during which the sutra has been transmitted, one of the most fascinating aspects of the chanted version is the similarities in the sounds of the mantra portion. Laborious textual comparison of texts and of rhymes in poems can (possibly) approximate ancient pronunciations of what was once written in India, in Sanskrit, but no one can ever know exactly how the mantra was originally pronounced. Nonetheless, when vocalized in different languages, it is usually recognizable, even if the rest of the sutra is not.

Oddly, the modern Mandarin Chinese pronunciation of the mantra seems to have diverged the most, for the first syllables—the *gaté gaté* or *gyatei gyatei* part (rendered in Sino-Chinese characters as 羯諦羯諦)—are often pronounced *jiédì jiédì*. Some divergence is to be anticipated, since in much of East Asia the Chinese *hanzi*, or ideograms, do not always have a single, fixed pronunciation; they really represent more of a mental concept than a single sound. People chanting a written Chinese version of the Heart Sutra are thus liable to pronounce it with the sounds they associate with the ideograms, and given the number of wildly different dialects in Chinese these pronunciations may also diverge wildly. But why the modern Mandarin version of the mantra, in particular, should be such an outlier long baffled me, because the Cantonese pronunciation of the mantra adheres fairly closely to that of other languages. The most cogent theory I have heard (in Cantonese-speaking Hong Kong) is that Cantonese is a far older form of Chinese, and Mandarin—at least as a unifying national language—is relatively new, dating back only to the early twentieth century.[12]

A DEEPER LOOK

The Heart Sutra mantra thus remains a sonic bridge among diverse languages and cultures, one that has survived nearly intact for over 1,400 years. And it has survived because it is a mantra. The *Oxford English Dictionary* defines a mantra as something originally Sanskrit, and

> A sacred text or passage, esp. one from the Vedas used as a prayer or incantation; a word or phrase from a sacred text repeated this way. Also, a holy name, for inward meditation.[13]

In the Buddhist world, mantras closely resemble, even overlap, with what are called *dhāraṇī*, or summaries of a longer, important text. Both of them are in a way a mnemonic aid in invoking the longer text, even though their usage in English literature is often confusing. In the Heart Sutra what is referred to by scholars variously as the mantra (and sometimes even the *dhāraṇī*) is only the last couple of lines of the entire sutra (only 18 out of around 260 ideograms in the Chinese version), but it can also be seen as the focus and crystallization of the entire sutra, which in itself is a reference to the power of the entire Prajñāpāramitā body of sutras. As the 14th Dalai Lama argues in his book *Essence of the Heart Sutra*, the entire sutra—the Heart of the Perfection of Wisdom, or the *Prajñāpāramitā Hṛdaya*, even the Perfection of Wisdom, presumably including the entire body of sutras—can be considered a type of mantra, and this is clearly spelled out with great force in the sutra itself.[14] If this is all confusing, it is important to remember that in Tibet and in some eras in Southeast Asia (such as ancient Java and even Cambodia), "Prajñāpāramitā" itself has at times been personified in statues and worshiped as a female deity.

Mantras can also be a type of magical spell. And because of their sacred, sound-based quality the words themselves usually have no meaning and, even if they do, tend not to be translated. In fact, some argue that even if a mantra has meaning it should *not* be translated. Thus, in the commentary that accompanies one English translation of the Heart Sutra, the twentieth-century Chinese Master Tanxu (1875–1963) is quoted as saying,

> "The Mantra belongs to the esoteric tradition and,
> accordingly, belongs to the five kinds of texts deemed
> primal, untranslatable, and inconceivable; when
> they are translated and explained, they will become
> conceivable Dharma, and their original meaning and
> merit will be lost."[15]

Despite this, nearly all modern scholars and Buddhist luminaries who translate the Heart Sutra into English at least attempt a translation of the mantra portion. For reference, some diligent scholars even include the Sanskrit Devanagari script, which is often assumed to be the original language of the sutra. But we have no reason to believe that Buddha delivered sermons in Sanskrit (which even in his era was a classical written language understood by few ordinary people). Most transliterate, or attempt to reproduce the sound of—rather than translate the original meaning of—the Sanskrit mantra in the Heart Sutra into the Roman alphabet, perhaps because most other mantras do not have meaning. They thus render the mantra as *gaté gaté pāragaté pārasaṃgaté bodhi svāhā*. And then, either as part of an official translation or an explanation or in footnotes, they give a modern English translation. Only occasionally do translators leave out the Sanskrit version of the mantra entirely and just give the translation.

I am fascinated by translations of the Heart Sutra mantra because, as noted (and unusual for mantras), it is not just a magical sound; it does have meaning. But in East Asian countries where ideograms (instead of alphabets) are used, this gets a bit tricky—especially in greater China and Japan where the Heart Sutra is most popular. Most of the eighteen characters assigned to the sutra's mantra portion are not individually used for their meaning but for an approximation of the assumed Sanskrit pronunciation. And given the nature of ideograms this becomes very difficult. A modern Chinese or Japanese person glancing casually at the mantra ideograms in isolation for the first time might see echoes of references to a castrated sheep, an ethnic group in China, some indication of truth, abandonment, a monk, or a Bodhisattva. The characters represent, in other words, a Chinese monk's attempt around fourteen hundred years ago to represent what he thought was a sound uttered by Buddhists in northeastern India (in a completely different language) nearly two thousand five hundred years ago. And as we have already seen, given that written Chinese normally uses ideograms with a largely pictorial meaning (instead of a fixed phonetic sound), wildly divergent pronunciations can arise unless there is some sort of pronunciation key. Fairly early on, the Japanese (followed by the Koreans) developed phonetic scripts that helped improve literacy and could effectively lock-in pronunciations of Chinese characters—but not so the Chinese themselves, who had to deal with so many different dialects.

Assuming that in ancient Sanskrit the mantra really did sound something like *gaté gaté pāragaté pārasaṃgaté bodhi svāhā*, those who were first to translate it into English heard something very different, depending on *where* they first heard it. Samuel Beal (1824–89), a British scholar of Chinese who translated the Heart Sutra in 1863, was primarily familiar with Cantonese since he had spent time in the British Navy after it seized Hong Kong in the First Opium War of 1842. In China then, he noted, "It is found in every temple, and very frequently in the interior of the small 'idols' (Josses) that garnish the domestic altars." To him, the mantra portion of the sutra that he heard in Chinese temples sounded like

Ki-tai, Ki-tai,
Po-lo, Ki-tai,
Po-lo-seng-Kitai,
Bo-tai-sah-po-ho.

At the end of his translation, he noted that in Sanskrit the same mantra would have been pronounced something like "*Gati, Gati, Para gati, Parasangati, Bodhisatvah,*" adding that they were "words I cannot attempt to explain." In 1875, when he later published his translation in a book on Buddhism, however, he did include a translation in a footnote:

> *Gone! gone! gone-across! (or burnt out) gone across for ever!) Bodhisatwa.*[16]

Six years later, in 1881, a German-born naturalized British citizen named F. Max Müller (1823–1900) added his take on the same mantra. Müller was a respected scholar of Sanskrit and (working from what was thought to be an ancient Sanskrit palm-leaf copy found in Japan's Hōryū-ji temple) on a single page he reproduced the original Sanskrit mantra text in Devanagari script on one side with an English translation of it on the other, rendering the mantra as:

> *O wisdom, gone, gone, gone to the other shore, landed at the other shore, Svâhâ!* [17]

From that point on, translations of the mantra became more and more refined, with only a few words of difference between them. In 1935, when the aforementioned Daisetsu Teitarō Suzuki translated the sutra into English for his 1935 *Manual of Zen Buddhism*, had he rendered the mantra in romanized Japanese its pronunciation would have sounded quite like Sanskrit, as *gyatei gyatei haragyatei hara sōgyatei boji sowaka*. Conscious of its etymology, perhaps, he rendered it in transliterated Sanskrit form and then (in parentheses) included an

English translation with two Sanskrit words retained, perhaps for "authenticity" or "power."

> *O Bodhi, gone, gone, gone to the other shore, landed at the other shore, Svaha!*[18]

In 1958, in his popular book *Buddhist Wisdom*, the brilliant linguist and scholar of Mahayana Buddhism, Edward Conze, included a translation of the Heart Sutra. He based it on his studies of ancient texts in multiple languages (mainly Sanskrit, but also Chinese, Japanese, Tibetan, and so on). He included not only transliterated Sanskrit but a completely English version to produce what has today become a classic English rendition of the sutra's concluding mantra:

> *Gone, gone, gone beyond, gone altogether beyond, O what an awakening, all-hail!*[19]

Much more recently, in 2005, the 14th Dalai Lama, working with a translator from Tibetan, while allowing that the mantra can be metaphorically read as "go to the other shore," rendered it on one page in transliterated Sanskrit and on an opposing page as:

> *Go, go, go beyond, go totally beyond, be rooted in the ground of enlightenment.*[20]

In 2014, the revered Vietnamese Zen master Thich Nhat Hanh issued a new translation of the Heart Sutra in his revised book *The Other Shore*. His English translation leaves the transliterated Sanskrit mantra but with a separate explanation elsewhere stating that it means:

> *Gone, gone, gone all the way over, everyone gone to the other shore, enlightenment, svāhā!*[21]

Among religious and secular scholars, and many non-tantric Buddhist practitioners, there has been a tendency to downplay the original magical component of the mantra, perhaps in an appeal to modern sensibilities. This has always puzzled me, since the sutra itself declares that the mantra is (as Conze translates it) "the great spell, the spell of great knowledge, the utmost spell, the unequalled spell, allayer of all suffering, in truth a supreme spell, the one and only spell."[22] In this regard, in his more recent rendition of the same section in the sutra, American translator Red Pine does us all a favor by using the phrase "mantra of great magic."[23]

In this vein, Donald S. Lopez Jr., professor of Buddhism and an expert on the sutra, wrote in a 1990 publication for the general public that the Sanskrit mantra itself occupies a special place in the sutra because it is

> ... in a language "entirely freed of the illusion of meaning." Without translation, there is "only the letter, and it is the truth of pure language, the truth as pure language," the pure language, called saṃskṛta. Untranslated, "language and revelation are one without any tension."[24]

So while most people around the world seem to enjoy

chanting the sutra in their native language, through some innate wisdom many chant the short and concluding powerful mantra—the transcendent magical spell that crystallizes the entire sutra— in a way that evokes the Sanskrit pronunciation. On YouTube, one can hear the beloved Hong Kong–based pop-singer/actress/diva Faye Wong, with the international Philharmonia of the Nations orchestra (conducted by Justus Frantz), sing a beautiful rendition of the Heart Sutra in Mandarin, not Cantonese. But whether singing the sutra in Hong Kong or mainland China, when she gets to the final mantra portion she renders it as close as possible to the Sanskrit pronunciation.

After observing Westerners chanting the mantra in Sanskrit, Kazuaki Tanahashi—translator, calligrapher, lecturer, and author of the 2014 book *The Heart Sutra: A Comprehensive Guide to the Classic of Mayahana Buddhism*—put it this way: "… there is something magical about reciting without fully understanding the words. This may be similar to the experience of people who love praying in Latin at Roman Catholic churches."[25]

And what is my own humble opinion? The mantra has power because it has meaning to those who recite it. And it has meaning because it has power, and the power is derived from Buddha, his disciples, the ancients, and a tradition that survives to this day.

3

Seeking Context

A copy of the Heart Sutra has hung on the wall over my bed over four decades now. It was written in brush and ink on ordinary *washi* paper, and I later had it mounted as a scroll on Japanese silk fabric backing. When the wind blows through the open window of my room, the wooden rod, or weight, at the bottom of the four-foot-long scroll often rattles gently against the wall. Because of this, over the years the scroll has developed a few creases and a tiny tear, but it is still remarkably unfaded, and its defects add what in Japan might be called a *wabi-sabi* aesthetic, which values imperfections and transience.

There are multiple original versions and translations of the Heart Sutra in existence. Sometimes the base versions are referred to by scholars as "recensions." There is a "longish" (but still very short) recension with a more standard Buddhist sutra introduction (beginning with "Thus I have heard. The Buddha was ...") and conclusion, and a shorter recension without it. The short version is generally agreed today by scholars to have been created before the long version, which may have been created later to give the sutra a more standard sutra format. There are also some minor variations, some with extraneous codas or preambles or titles added by various Buddhist sects. My hanging scroll is what might be thought of as the "universal" short version—by far the most popular throughout East Asia, and a nearly exact copy of what was either translated or compiled by (or at least attributed to) the famous Chinese monk Xuanzang in 649 CE, nearly one thousand four hundred years ago. It is, to me, what might be thought of as the "master copy." It is what I have long studied and memorized.

In Sino-Japanese, the Xuanzang version can be arranged into a variety of physical matrices. My hanging scroll is vertical in orientation and read from top to bottom, right to left, with the sutra title indicated at the beginning and abbreviated at the end. The body consists of 262 Sino-Japanese characters, or ideograms, arranged in a symmetrical matrix of eight lines of about 30 characters each, and one line of approximately 22. When recited in Japanese my sutra sounds radically different from how it sounds in other languages, but visually it is otherwise nearly identical to the Xuanzang "master copy," save for a few minor variations in ideograms and the number of strokes they contain. As Japanese Heart Sutra scholar/priest Fukui Fumimasa (Bunga) has noted in his extensive research on this issue, one of the few differences between Japanese and Chinese versions is that nearly all Japanese copies of the Heart Sutra have two extra ideograms (一切 or *issai* in Japanese, meaning "all" or "without exception" or simply an emphasis).[26] They come between the character strings 遠離 and 顛倒夢想, forming a phrase that can be translated as "Far beyond all inverted views."

Satoko's Heart Sutra. >

摩訶般若波羅蜜多心經

觀自在菩薩行深般若波羅蜜多時照見五蘊皆空度一切苦厄舍利子色不異空空不異色色即是空空即是色受想行識亦復如是舍利子是諸法空相不生不滅不垢不淨不增不減是故空中無色無受想行識無眼耳鼻舌身意無色聲香味觸法無眼界乃至無意識界無無明亦無無明盡乃至無老死亦無老死盡無苦集滅道無智亦無得以無所得故菩提薩埵依般若波羅蜜多故心無罣礙無罣礙故無有恐怖遠離一切顛倒夢想究竟涅槃三世諸佛依般若波羅蜜多故得阿耨多羅三藐三菩提故知般若波羅蜜多是大神咒是大明咒是無上咒是無等等咒能除一切苦真實不虛故說般若波羅蜜多咒即說咒曰羯諦羯諦波羅羯諦波羅僧羯諦菩提薩婆訶般若心經

七十七 字字子

The individual characters in my scroll are not perfect in their artistry, but they are well-formed and solid. Their precise positioning, in fact, suggests that they were rendered with a paper guide underneath that had a matrix of small empty boxes for each character. Nowadays, many people trace the characters themselves using special guides placed underneath the scroll paper, but given the era, and the calligrapher's age at the time, these characters were probably rendered from memory. The signature at the very end, customarily applied by the calligrapher who has executed the scroll, says 七十七歳を咲子 or "seventy-seven years old Satoko." The first two characters of her name (the *sa-to*) are written with what are called *hentaigana*, or unorthodox, abstracted ideograms as phonetics, an archaic style today occasionally used by calligraphers and almost no one else.

I first met Satoko in the winter of 1975–76, when visiting a friend's family in Ōichō, a tiny town in western Japan facing the Japan Sea. Satoko was dressed in an old-fashioned rural style and already seemed shrunken and wizened to me. My most vivid memory is of her kneeling on the tatami mats in the old, cold wooden house, carefully writing the entire Heart Sutra with brush and ink. It was part of her daily ritual, and the sutras that she copied were usually thrown away, since the act of creating the copy—not the end product itself—was the most important part of the ritual. When I asked for a copy, she was more than happy to give it to me and surprised that I would even want one. According to her granddaughter, Keiko, Satoko lived until ninety-six and continued her ritual until she was nearly ninety, adding that, "they say the older the calligrapher, the more value accrues from the copy of the Heart Sutra."

As I have learned, the Heart Sutra can be a string of thoughts, a rhythmical chant, a song, and, when rendered in text, even assume a physical form such as a scroll or countless other symbolic and decorative items. It can be examined with different degrees of semantic magnification, from the macro to the micro, and viewed from doctrinal, faith-based, academic, and personal perspectives. My goal has always been personal, not didactic, to understand the sutra better, to start by grasping its most basic structure and context. By locating it within Buddhism, it has also been my hope that I might understand Buddhism better, for the complexity of Buddhism has always made my mind spin. If Buddhism is like an infinitely layered onion, then surely the Heart Sutra is like a specialized tool to strip away layer upon layer, eventually reaching a type of liberation, or what Buddhists themselves might even call a state of "emptiness"—which is, as many people far more learned than I have pointed out, not at all what it seems.

Let's begin with this: The Heart Sutra is a Buddhist sutra. "Sutra" is an ancient Sanskrit word originally meaning a thread, string, or a "rule"; in a broader, modern context, it can be a mnemonic device that helps people memorize grammar, laws, or a philosophy. In Buddhism, however, sutra usually refers to what are assumed by believers to be the teachings of the Buddha, even the actual words of the Buddha. There are hundreds upon hundreds of Buddhist sutras. They are thus a type of sacred scripture, passed down orally for many centuries and then finally compiled in writing (and then, over the centuries, usually accompanied with official learned commentaries). The "heart" in the Heart Sutra—the *Hṛdaya* in the *Prajñāpāramitā Hṛdaya Sūtra*, or the "Heart of the Perfection of

Wisdom Sutra"—is prone to overinterpretation in English as a Christianized or romantic "heart," when in Sanskrit and Chinese it was probably closer to the words "essence" or "core." It is, in other words, the "essence" of the much older and larger Prajñāpāramitā sutras, the Perfection of Wisdom sutras, which contain thousands upon thousands of lines.

Although some sutras speak of myriads of cosmological past, present, and future Buddhas, the historical Buddha is believed to have lived in northeastern India (near today's Nepal) some 2,400~2,500 years ago. Referred to today variously as Siddhārtha Gautama, or Sakyamuni, only the most rudimentary outlines of his life are known. He was born a prince and raised in wealth and luxury but renounced his position and family. In a quest for truth and a solution to human suffering, he first became an ascetic, practicing many physically arduous but spiritual disciplines. Then, after some six years of searching, he found a "middle way," between self-gratification and self-mortification. And when meditating under the Bodhi tree in Bodh Gaya one day, he finally achieved enlightenment. Yet his real contribution lay not just in reaching enlightenment. It was also in telling others, in a sermon in Varanasi, about what he had realized, offering to those interested his teachings on what would become known as the Dharma, or truth or law.

Everything comes from something, and Buddhism grew out of the rich traditions of pre-Hindu Brahmanism, from the same fertile soil that produced today's Hinduism and Jainism, with which it shares much. But the monks who organized this religion stressed the Buddha; the Dharma, or "Cosmic Law"; and the Sangha, or monastic community. Buddhism was revolutionary in the sense that it downplayed the caste orientation and rituals of the then-contemporary Brahmanism. It could therefore appeal to people of any caste and any ethnic group—thus making it a potentially universal, if not revolutionary, faith. And perhaps because of this, Buddhism thereafter spread rapidly, far beyond the Indian subcontinent to Sri Lanka, Southeast Asia, Tibet, and most of East Asia. At one point it was even popular in what would be today's Indonesia, Afghanistan, and eastern Iran.

The goal of the Buddha's teachings was the elimination of suffering through extinction of the ego or sense of individuality, and an attainment of Nirvana and a break from the cycle of rebirth. The teachings provided a framework with which to achieve an understanding of an infinitely complex universe and to carry out a peaceful way of living. This framework could be a type of salvation. But beyond that, things get quite complicated, especially for me. The teachings were centered on concepts such as The Four Noble Truths and The Eightfold Path. In the mind-numbingly nested-list-prone world of Buddhism, the Four Noble Truths are, according to the 14th Dalai Lama (who speaks from a Tibetan tradition), "the truth of suffering, the truth of its origin, the truth of the possibility of its cessation, and the truth of the path that leads to that cessation." The Eightfold Path, on the other hand, is represented by right views, right thinking, right speech, right actions, right livelihood, right efforts, right mindfulness, and right concentration. Another important dharmic list—the five *skandhas*, or "aggregates" or "heaps—also plays an important part in the beginning of the Heart Sutra. The *skandhas* make up the personality and experience of an individual and, according to one dictionary of Buddhism, are materiality or form, sensations or feeling, perception or discrimination, conditioning factors, and consciousness.[27]

On the Indian subcontinent—the land of its birth—Buddhism has today been almost entirely supplanted by Hinduism and Islam (although I have heard some Indians claim that Buddhism is really a subset of Hinduism). And its originally monastery-centered structure and emphasis on peaceful meditation may have given it a distinct disadvantage in the face of the more aggressive Islam, for it has been eliminated in today's Afghanistan, Iran, and Indonesia. Still, it remains one of the major religions of the world, even though—perhaps because it often downplays worship of a "god" or "gods," at a high level considering them almost irrelevant—in the West there is sometimes even what I see as a silly debate as to whether it should be called a philosophy instead of a religion. In academic circles, because it does not assert the existence of a creator, as do Christianity, Judaism, Islam, and Hinduism, it is often called a "nontheistic" religion.

Just as there are many different sects in the monotheistic, Abrahamic religions of Judaism, Christianity, and Islam, there are scores if not hundreds of different sects in Buddhism. Many offer entirely different views of how to achieve Nirvana or Enlightenment, and some even argue that it is impossible to achieve them anyway or disagree on their definition. One could say that modern Buddhism is like a river of thought that emanated from one person. After being expounded and commented and expanded upon by disciples and countless students over nearly two and a half millennia, the thoughts of the Buddha have forked into different subchannels, forming remarkably different schools and sects, many with very different practices. There is no monolithic "Buddhism," and in the Western world, where images of Buddhism have often been formed from the influence of Japanese Zen and Theosophist sects, it might come as a surprise to know that most ordinary Buddhists do not do *zazen* or even meditate daily, leaving that to the monks and nuns or the ultradedicated and instead—as in most religions—simply try to adhere to general Buddhist principles in their lives.

One important difference between the Abrahamic religions and Buddhism is that Buddhism has never had a centralized figure such as a pope (or even a "God" or creator-figure), or a single Bible or Torah or Koran to serve as a master reference. Instead, an inherent tolerance in ideology, and hundreds and hundreds of different sutras, have allowed a highly organic and complex branching evolution of beliefs.

Still, generalizations can be made. Mahayana Buddhists often refer to "three turnings of the wheel of the dharma" in the evolution of their religion. The first was Buddha's lectures at Deer Park in Sārnāth, in India, when he introduced the Four Noble Truths and the Eightfold Path to his disciples. The second was an emphasis on the "perfection of wisdom," and the elaboration of the concept of "emptiness." And the third was the teaching of Buddha's final or true intention, in the form of the Yogācāra doctrine, which covers, among other things, the illusory and dependency-related nature of reality.[28]

The Heart Sutra sits firmly within the second turning of the wheel, during the early stages of what has become known as Mahayana Buddhism. The Mahayana school emerged many centuries after the historical Buddha and today is widely practiced in China, Japan, Vietnam, Mongolia, Korea, and Tibet (although Tibetan Buddhist sects also combine tantric/esoteric and other beliefs as well). It is a radical departure from the older, pre-Mahayana schools, such as the Nikaya or what are sometimes referred to as the Theravada or occasionally even the Hinayana schools, which are practiced today in Sri Lanka and much of Southeast Asia.[29]

The Mahayana school is characterized by an emphasis on Bodhisattvas, or saint-like beings who, while capable of reaching Nirvana, out of compassion stay in this world to help others. By far the greatest number of Buddhists are members of one or another Mahayana sects in East Asia. And the Heart Sutra is most definitely in the Mahayana tradition.

SUTRA, STRUCTURE, AND LOGIC

While writing this book, I opened a footlocker in my garage that holds some old academic records. It's a locker unopened for decades. I had nearly forgotten, but in the spring of 1972, after a two-year sojourn at a Japanese university, I took a class at the University of California, Santa Barbara, just before graduating. It was titled "Religious Studies 164A, Buddhism in South Asia," taught by Professor Gerald J. Larson. I recall little of it, except that at twenty-two I was completely bewildered and lost by most of what was presented—especially the long lists of unfamiliar Buddhist concepts and terms. I remember feeling at the time that I didn't have enough intellectual candlepower or patience for this sort of thing. Remarkably, given how little I remember, is that in my old report card I found that I earned the grade of B. Moreover, among the class notes I unearthed from that period—dusty, hand-scrawled, now nearly illegible, and almost half a century old—I was surprised to discover that we had even been given a handout of Edward Conze's translation of the Heart Sutra—that I had in fact seen this even before hearing Allen Ginsberg recite it. It was mimeographed, with purple text. And next to a transliterated version of the mantra I had scrawled a note, saying, "This is it—all there is to know." But whether I was referring to the mantra or to the entire sutra, I can't tell now. What I do remember from that class is not the Heart Sutra copy but Nāgārjuna's Four-Fold Negative Dialectic. As I scrawled in my notes in somewhat disjointed fashion,

> [He] wants to get into every view and show its irrationality in its own framework. He does this by means of the Four-Fold Negative Dialectic, which says that (1) a thing neither is (2) nor is not (3) nor both is and is not (4) nor neither is nor is not. These are the only possibilities with respect to any view…. Empirical phenomenological "truths" exist but we can't account metaphysically for the ideas…. All metaphysics are impossible.

I found this sort of super-reductive logic memorable mainly because it seemed completely novel and ridiculous (not to mention overly intellectual). Yet in the context of the Heart Sutra I see now that it fits, and that the sutra fits especially well within what Nāgārjuna is really most famous for, which is his concept of *śūnyatā*, or what is often translated as "emptiness." And *śūnyatā*, in turn, is at the core of the Mahayana school of Buddhism and especially the Heart Sutra. It's an idea that hints at the relativistic and illusory nature of our reality, and as most writers on Buddhism will eagerly remind us, takes a very, very, very long time to understand fully.

Nāgārjuna was an Indian philosopher who lived centuries after the Buddha, perhaps in the second century CE. He is a towering figure in Mahayana Buddhism, regarded by some as a "second Buddha." According to the *Princeton Dictionary of Buddhism*, he is noted, among other things, for his concepts of "emptiness" and being a proponent of Mahayana teachings, in particular the *madhyamaka*, or "middle way," which charts a path between the extremes of eternalism and annihilation, or existence and nonexistence. But so little is known about him that he is also a good illustration of the organic evolution of Buddhism and of the mixture of legend and myth and folk beliefs that infuse many aspects of its various schools today. He is said, according to one legend, to have "retrieved from the Dragon King's palace at the bottom of the sea the 'Perfection of Wisdom in One Hundred Thousand Lines'...," which the Buddha had entrusted to the undersea king of the serpent-like *nāgas* for safekeeping.[30] And this "Perfection of Wisdom," or Prajñāpāramitā, is what the Heart Sutra—the "Heart of the Perfection of Wisdom Sutra"—is all about.

One of the reasons the Heart Sutra may be confusing is well expressed by Karl Brunnhölzl, a renowned Buddhist translator of Tibetan and author of the insightful and witty commentary-book titled *The Heart Attack Sūtra*:

> What we can say about the *Heart Sūtra* is that it is completely crazy. If we read it, it does not make any sense.... When we read it, it sounds nuts, but that is actually where the wisdom part comes in.

Yet Brunnhölzl's focus is on the Tibetan and Sanskrit versions, and the "long-form" version, of the Heart Sutra.[31] The short-form universal version of Xuanzang—that of my hanging scroll and the world's most popular format—is regarded today by most scholars as having been created before the long form. And because it is so short, it could be said to be even more opaque and even harder to understand.

The "long-form" version of the Heart Sutra popular in Tibet and other regions begins with the line "Thus I have heard," common to most Buddhist sutras. The setting is established as Vulture Peak in today's state of Bihar in India, where presumably the Buddha is lecturing, with a great assembly of ordained monks and Bodhisattvas. The principals may be the Buddha; the Buddha's disciple, Śāriputra, who asks the questions; and Avalokiteśvara, who answers them. But the short Xuanzang version of the Heart Sutra does not even tell us this directly. In it, there are just two characters, Avalokiteśvara and Śāriputra, and only the former is "speaking."

Avalokiteśvara—in Sanskrit meaning the "one who gazes down, with compassion, or empathy"—is the Bodhisattva who has resolved to save all sentient beings from suffering in this world and is the most widely worshiped Bodhisattva in all of Buddhism. The popular name for Avalokiteśvara in East Asia is Guanyin in Chinese, Chenrezig in Tibetan, and Kannon in Japanese and is written in Chinese and Japanese with the ideograms 観音 for "Observing the Sound" (of the world). But in the Xuanzang Heart Sutra this Bodhisattva is represented with the ideograms 観自在, or the one who "sees freely or unfettered." Capable of traveling through time and space and appearing to different people in a myriad of different forms, Avalokiteśvara

TOP LEFT: Early-twelfth-century Guanyin, Bodhisattva of Compassion from Chinese Jin dynasty. (Photo courtesy Boston Museum of Fine Arts, Hervey Edward Wetzel Fund.)   TOP RIGHT: Giant Kannon bust at Ofuna, near Kamakura. Completed in 1960, 25m tall.   BOTTOM: Modern Guanyin, Bodhisattva of Compassion, in front of Heart Sutra at Fo Guang Shan Buddha Museum, 2018.

was originally a male figure in India, but over the centuries in China s/he morphed into a largely female one, usually depicted in statuary and paintings in graceful, peaceful, and sometimes even sensuous form. In modern-day Japan and China, stupendously huge Avalokiteśvara statues sometimes resemble the depictions of the Catholic Mother Mary, with a cowl. As can be seen at the 26 Martyrs Museum in Japan's Nagasaki, during the more than two hundred years during which Christianity was forbidden in Japan on penalty of death, underground or "hidden" Christians occasionally even worshiped tiny Guanyin statues from China as a substitute for the Blessed Virgin, the object of their real devotion. Yet there are many different styles of Avalokiteśvara/Guanyin/Kannon images and sometimes s/he has a slightly unsettling eleven heads and hundreds of arms.

At least one form of Avalokiteśvara icon may be very familiar to non-believers. In the West, and in North American middle-class gardens, one is likely to find—along with stone statues of serenely meditating Buddhas—the sinuous but kindly female Avalokiteśvara, with only one head and two arms.

The other main character in the Heart Sutra is the listener, Śāriputra, said to have been the wisest of Buddha's ten disciples. A former Brahmin who is also said to have died before the Buddha, his name appears twice in the sutra as he is addressed by Avalokiteśvara about the perfection of wisdom, almost in a lecturing tone.

Even without pondering the Heart Sutra's core meaning, the scroll on my wall has what appears, to me at least, to have an obvious four-part structure. There is (1) a very short introduction, describing how Avalokiteśvara was meditating on the perfection of wisdom, when s/he realized that all five

Modern sculpture of the wisest disciple, Śāriputra, by Nakamura Shinya. (Photo courtesy Paramita Museum. © Nakamura Shinya.)

of the aforementioned *skandhas* are all empty. Then there follows (2) a lengthy declaration by Avalokiteśvara, almost in an admonition to the diligent Śāriputra, of what this all means and the nature of reality. Then there is (3) a heralding of the mantra. And finally (4), the mantra itself is revealed and proclaimed.

There are many ways to view the structure of the sutra, and indeed academics and religious scholars argue regularly about this. And they have also debated for years as to whether the most important part of the sutra is what I would call the declaration and explanation (2), or the mantra itself (4). Japanese authority Fukui, mentioned earlier, thinks of the Chinese version of the sutra as having eight logical sections primarily delineated by the character 故 (meaning "therefore," "hence," or "because") and he believes that for centuries the mantra was actually the most important part and that only much later did the declaration about the nature of reality—or the "emptiness" section—come to be regarded as the focus of the sutra, since it encapsulates some of the underpinnings of the Mahayana school of Buddhism.[32]

Immediately after the sutra's very short twenty-five-character introduction that "sets the stage," Avalokiteśvara begins his declaration to Śāriputra, commencing with what are arguably the most famous lines, usually translated along the lines of:

> Form is not different from emptiness; emptiness is
> not different from form; form is emptiness; and emp-
> tiness is form.

This is followed by what seems like a long series of negatives and double negatives deconstructing nearly all aspects of human reality and reflecting much of the negative dialectics of the pioneering Mahayana figure Nāgārjuna. In my hanging scroll, for example, the Sino/Japanese ideograms 無 ("nothingness" or a negation, sometimes also written as 无) and 不 ("no or not") occur over thirty times. And partly because of this, nearly every English book on the Heart Sutra is careful to emphasize that the sutra (and Buddhism by extension) is *not*, contrary to all appearances, nihilistic. What really is at work here is an exotic system of logic used in Mahayana Buddhism, and especially in the Prajñāpāramitā sutras, described by famous Zen philosopher D. T. Suzuki as 即非の論理 (*sokuhi no ronri),* or the "Logic of Affirmation-in-Negation." When I was confused, Mark Blum, Buddhist Studies professor at the University of California, Berkeley, and something of an expert on the subject, once valiantly tried to explain it to me in modern terms:

> The core idea is that any and all assertions need to be negated before they are affirmed and that negation functions as a form of affirmation.... If we do not do this, the direct affirmation that most people do will inevitably include, often unwittingly, prejudicial thinking based on past knowledge, past perception, past realities, etc., when the fact of impermanence shows us that everything is different at every moment.... Thus the buddha and buddhism must be negated to be recognized as real. The process is what the Donovan song was trying to say: first there is a mountain, then there is no mountain, then there is.[33]

In my scroll, the ideogram 空, often translated as "emptiness," appears over seven times, and it, too, can amplify an impression of nothingness or nihilism. Pronounced *kū* in Japanese and *kong* in Mandarin, it represents the Sanskrit word *śūnyatā* or *śūnya*. Many modern translators often go to great lengths to avoid using the term "emptiness," but this is not easy. There are some seductive long definitions. In the wonderful online *Digital Dictionary of Buddhism*, Charles Muller and Jimmy Yu define 空 in its most common usage as

> [T]he distinctive Mahāyāna Buddhist view of the character of all existence, wherein all phenomena are

understood to arise in dependence upon each other, and thus there is no phenomenon that has independent, determinable, or permanent existence; nor do any phenomena possess any sort of unchanging inner nature (自性). This means that the everyday conceptions that we have of the existence of ourselves and the objects around us as concrete entities are inaccurate, as the determinations we make of ourselves and objects are arbitrary conceptual reifications.[34]

There are of course much shorter definitions. As noted in the *Princeton Dictionary of Buddhism*, "emptiness" in Mahayana Buddhism is actually neither nothingness nor the absence of existence, but the absence of a falsely imagined type of existence.[35] Still, in translations of the Heart Sutra, a single word must usually suffice (perhaps with footnotes or commentary) to represent the illusory nature of what we perceive as reality. In lieu of "emptiness," some modern translators have used "voidness." And there is always a temptation to use "zero," because the Sanskrit *śūnya* can also have that meaning. D. T. Suzuki, in his 1934 translation of the Heart Sutra, used "emptiness" but tried to cover himself in a supplemental note:

When Buddhists declare all things to be empty, they are not advocating a nihilistic view; on the contrary an ultimate reality is hinted at, which cannot be subsumed under the categories of logic. With them, to proclaim the conditionality of things is to point to the existence of something altogether unconditioned and transcendent of all determination. Sunyata may thus often be most appropriately rendered by the Absolute.[36]

In 2014, the author Kazuaki Tanahashi included a new English translation (done with Joan Halifax) of the Heart Sutra in his book, using the word "boundlessness," which I like.[37] But one of my favorites in the "non-emptiness" category is from Samuel Beal's 1865 translation from the Chinese, where he uses the word "space." Since the same ideogram 空 today, in both Chinese and Japanese, is also often used in compounds related to air or sky or outer space, this makes a certain weird sense, at least to me.[38]

In studying the sutra on my wall, I'm also fascinated by the way the original Xuanzang version uses both transliterated and translated terminology, the first to represent sound and the second to represent meaning. The ideograms for Avalokiteśvara appear only once, as does that for Buddha (佛), the latter in reference to Buddhas of the "three worlds," or the past, present, and future. The characters for Śāriputra, to whom Avalokiteśvara is speaking, are used twice, not translated, but transliterated. *Prajñāpāramitā* is also not translated, but transliterated, and it appears five times, which makes sense since that is the subject of the Heart Sutra. The *bodhi* in Bodhisattva, which means "awakening," is also not translated, but transliterated, and it appears three times. Although profound Buddhist concepts are probably embedded in nearly every character in the sutra, one of the longest strings of ideograms in the body of the text (a true mouthful and most difficult to understand for a novice like me, or for modern Chinese and Japanese) is also a transliteration, the 阿耨多羅三藐三菩提, a representation of the Sanskrit *anuttarā-samyak-saṃbodhi*, namely, the "unsurpassed, complete, and perfect enlightenment, or the enlightenment of a Buddha, superior to all other forms of enlightenment."[39] For ancient Chinese translators, it was apparently easier to simply assign ideograms to approximate the Sanskrit of some terms rather than render their meaning in Chinese.

Memorizing the Heart Sutra is not easy in any language. One Japanese friend, an ordained priest in the Japanese Koyasan Shingon sect, told me that it's best not to even try to understand the Heart Sutra intellectually in the beginning, but just to learn to chant it and absorb it, letting the vibrations seep through one's body, almost like learning a song. Other Japanese books in my possession recommend, rather than trying to understand it, simply copying the sutra as a meditative ritual. And the sutra hanging on my wall makes this memorization a tad easier since, like many modern Japanese and Chinese versions, it has tiny circles marking character strings, almost like a type of punctuation. Classical Chinese often used no punctuation, so this helps establish a sense of rhythm and provides logical breaks in what is otherwise an unbroken string of ideograms. It is one of the main differences between my scroll and classic versions authored in China nearly 1,400 years ago.

Today, when I read the sutra, the experience is almost like reciting it and in my mind seems akin to hearing a grand piece of classical music. I imagine a symphony, in four movements, starting with a very brief but slow and quiet introduction, then moving forcefully but calmly into the long explanatory section, then a louder, more forceful declaration stage, and finally a crescendo, the climax, as it were, of the mantra itself, followed by sudden, expanding silence.

4

Xuanzang

In 2007, at a shop in Guangzhou City, I watched as an extraordinarily dexterous calligrapher demonstrated his skills. He could write famous phrases and poems and even compose poems when requested in beautiful brush strokes, holding his brush in his mouth, his left hand, or his right hand. And sometimes he would write with one brush in each hand at the same time. He had on display beside him a page from a "Who's Who" book, listing himself as "a very important" person named Xian Zhang. On the wall behind him hung samples of his work, the most recent ones still drying, the process speeded up by a young female assistant with a portable blow dryer. He was a one-man tourist attraction, and when I saw that he had a copy of the Heart Sutra displayed on the wall behind him, I asked him if he would do the mantra portion for me, which he obligingly did, using both hands.

Whenever I have visited mainland China, or anywhere in the Chinese diaspora, I have always been on the lookout for examples of the Heart Sutra in use. China is where the most popular translation (or version), attributed to the monk Xuanzang in 649, emerged and became deeply ingrained in society until the 1949 revolution. Shortly after fleeing the mainland for Hong Kong in 1950, popular writer Xu Xu (1908–80), hinted at its popularity among ordinary folk, reminiscing in a short story called "Bird Talk" about a mesmerizing but perhaps mildly autistic young woman in prerevolution days. She had just been introduced to the Heart Sutra by a teacher in a countryside Buddhist convent the previous day.

> "Did you like the Heart Sutra?" I asked.
> "Yes," she said, her face shining with a marvelous radiance. "I can already recite it from memory. It's even more interesting than poetry."
> "You can already recite it from memory?" I asked in surprise.
> "How about I'll recite it for you? And she began to recite fluently. Her low murmur again was imbued with a marvelous beauty.
> I was in awe.[40]

Needless to say, after 1949 the revolution suppressed most religious activities. Over seventy years later, the modern Communist Chinese government is still officially atheist and has a well-earned international reputation for religious repression. But today a unique medley of religious and quasi-religious beliefs are tolerated, even government-sanctioned. They include Buddhism, Confucianism, Taoism, Christianity, folk religions, and Islam. The first three groups, being deeply entrenched in traditional Chinese culture, have the advantage in that they can be used to enhance a burgeoning nationalism. Big exceptions today are anything regarded as too independent

Xuanzang statue in Xi'an.

and a threat to the Party, such as Islam linked to an independence movement in the heavily Muslim and restive Xinjiang area in the west, the quasi-Buddhist/Taoist/Confucian Falun Gong cult, and any forms of Tibetan Buddhism with connections to the 14th Dalai Lama. Thus, as the aforementioned Professor Blum of Berkeley notes,

> The Party needs a "safe" form of religion that will not upset the status quo, and Buddhism plays that role better than anyone. That is, as long as the independence streak in the Buddhist tradition is kept at bay, either from self-imposed discipline or from intimidation by The Party.[41]

As domestic tourism has exploded in China, so, too, have visits to famous Buddhist sites by ordinary tourists and religious pilgrims. My own visits have include the remote Dunhuang grottos, ancient caves filled with Buddhist paintings, where some of the oldest versions of the Heart Sutra have been discovered; the 233-foot-tall, giant Maitreya at Leshan, now said to be the largest Buddha statue in the world in the wake of the Taliban's destruction of the monoliths in Afghanistan's Bamiyan; the golden Samantabhadra Bodhisattva statue on top of Mt. Emei, one of four sacred Buddhist peaks in China; and the Giant Wild Goose Pagoda in Xi'an, originally dedicated to the sutras and artifacts brought back from India by the renowned translator Xuanzang. One sight I haven't seen but would love to see is the new Nanjing Niushou Mountain Cultural Tourism Zone—an ancient-modern merger of world Buddhist culture and modern architecture, where part of what

Giant Wild Goose Pagoda in Xi'an.

is said to be the Buddha's skull is on display in an extraordinarily lavish setting. The crowds at some of these sights have to be seen to be believed. When I visited Leshan, there were so many boats in the rivers below the giant Buddha, vying to get a good view of it, that the boat we were on was nearly rammed by accident.

At many larger Buddhist temples in China today it is hard to ignore the Heart Sutra, even if the sutra is not a central focus. One example is the sprawling Guiyuan Temple complex that I once visited in the city of Wuhan in Hubei Province. It has thousands of tourists and devotees and monks. Guiyuan was founded in 1658 and (as is often the case in China) has been destroyed and rebuilt multiple times. It is a Chan (Zen) sect temple that dates back to the sixth century and is the parent of what is known as Sōtō Zen in Japan. In this tradition, the monks chant the Heart Sutra regularly as part of their morning sutra practice. Some of the halls have banners and walls with the Heart Sutra embroidered or inscribed. In one hall, amid icons of Buddhas and Arhat sages on display, there is an icon of the "narrator" of the Heart Sutra—Avalokiteśvara—with a "thousand arms." Outside, there is an especially imposing sixty-foot-tall, twenty-ton brass statue of him/her, with two frontal aspects, back-to-back, allowing a 360-degree world view. While not viewable when I visited, inside the grounds is a special depository of sacred Buddhist texts and objects, including a unique miniature copy of the Heart Sutra.

Around many temples in China, one can often buy CDs with the sound of the Heart Sutra being chanted or rosaries with Xuanzang's version of the Heart Sutra inscribed in tiny characters. Printed or calligraphic copies may be sold of the sutra, and sometimes it is also inscribed on narrow bamboo or wooden slats called *zhu jian* (as ancient sutras in China often were). At the huge, cavernous, ultra-high-speed "bullet train" stations, I have been fascinated to see ordinary bookstores—heavily regulated by the government—selling books on religion and especially on Buddhism and the Heart Sutra.

Some of the most telling signs of a newly awakened Chinese interest in Buddhism come from outside the mainland. The popular Taiwan sect, Fo Guang Shan, stresses "Humanistic Buddhism." As the *New York Times* reported on June 24, 2017, by playing down the religious aspects of its message and stressing "traditional Chinese culture," it has been able to make considerable inroads into the mainland, opening cultural centers in major cities where sutras, including the Heart Sutra, can be read, and building a giant temple on the outskirts of Yixing, in southern Jiangsu Province, not too far from Shanghai.[42] When I visited the sprawling Fo Guang Shan monastery and museum complex in Kaohsiung, Taiwan, I could not fail to notice a photo prominently displayed of the sect's aging founder, Hsing Yun, shaking hands with mainland China's life-long president and head of the Communist Party, Xi Jingping.

Further indications of change come from even further away, even outside the Chinese diaspora. In Japan, Yakushiji Kanhō, who goes by the stage name Kissaquo, performs a musical "chorus" version of the Heart Sutra and uses social media to promote his recordings and concerts. A thoroughly modern vice-abbot of the Rinzai Zen sect, his performances have been extremely popular in Japan. To his surprise, he found that he had an even bigger audience in mainland China, that people there were logging in to watch videos of his performance in huge numbers—over twenty million—mainly on social media sites like Weibo and WeChat. This led him to start touring not only in Taiwan but in Hong Kong and cities in mainland China. Given the nationalistic enmity sometimes fostered by the Chinese government against Japan in recent years, this is a remarkable development, especially since Kissaquo sings/chants the Heart Sutra on stage in China in Japanese, not Chinese. In 2020 his stated goal on his website (in Japanese and Chinese), was to "create connections between Japan and Asia and to continue to convey Buddhism by putting it into sound." According to his general manager, Ogawa Mayumi, he feels that the people who come to his concerts in China are even more comfortable worshiping than in Japan. When he sings the Heart Sutra many in the audience even put their palms together in prayer with him.[43]

Another unexpected outside connection is the series of books published in America by Bill Porter, the aforementioned "Red Pine." Porter is a translator of Chinese poetry and Buddhist texts, including the Heart Sutra (with his own commentaries), and a charismatic exponent of Zen with an unusual background. The son of a convicted bank robber but later honestly wealthy-then-bankrupt father, he was once a resident for several years at Fo Guang Shan and other monasteries in Taiwan. Now living in Port Townsend, Washington, as he confessed to me, until recently his years of toil kept him partially reliant on food stamps to support his family. Now many of his books have been back-translated into Chinese and—despite continuing restrictions on religion in China—they are selling vastly more copies than they ever did in English, allowing him to own his own home.[44]

SEEKING THE TRUTH

Buddhism was introduced into China primarily via Central Asia by intrepid missionaries from India beginning in the Han dynasty nearly two thousand years ago (only four or five centuries after the death of the historical Buddha). In China, Mahayana Buddhism—with its emphasis on Bodhisattvas and salvation—soon became dominant, and it is from this school that the Prajñāpāramitā sutras, and eventually the Heart Sutra, emerged. Yet for Buddhism to spread, translations of Indian sutras from Sanskrit into Chinese were necessary, and they, too, were produced very early, even in the second century. While copies of some early translations exist, the original Sanskrit texts from India—on which the translations were based—all today have mostly been lost. This is likely because most were written on palm leaves, which did not survive the Indian subcontinent climate, wars, and religious upheavals and crackdowns, not to mention the arduous journey to China. Ancient copies of the Heart Sutra exist not only in Sanskrit but in Tibetan, Mongolian, and many other translations, but as of this date Chinese "translations" of the Heart Sutra remain the oldest credible copies found anywhere.

Eight translated Chinese versions of the Heart Sutra are included in the *Taishō Tripiṭaka*, compiled in Japan in the early twentieth century and one of the most comprehensive collections of the surviving Chinese Buddhist canon. As usual, arguments among scholars have raged about the provenance of some of the earliest versions. One example is a version long thought to have been translated by the famous monk, missionary, and translator Kumārajīva at the end of the fourth century.

From the Buddhist kingdom of Kucha, along the Silk Road

on the northern edge of the Taklamakan desert, Kumārajīva became a convert to the Mahayana school and was especially influenced by Nāgārjuna's thought. He studied in Kashmir but later in life became fluent in Chinese. And in Chang'an, or today's Xi'an, China, with a team of others under his direction, he began translating many of the major Prajñāpāramitā sutras. His ability to find appropriate Chinese ideograms to substitute for arcane Buddhist concepts in Sanskrit texts won him wide acclaim—so much so that the "accuracy of his translations is said to be attested by the fact that his tongue remained unburned during his cremation."[45] At least one Korean international Zen sect, the Kwan Um School, still uses a version of what they claim is Kumārajīva's translation of the Heart Sutra.[46]

Yet among many prominent scholars of Buddhism today, what was long believed to have been Kumārajīva's translation of the Heart Sutra is now held in dispute, partly because of the lack of contemporary commentaries on it. Professor Watanabe Shōgo of Toyo University in Japan, for example, now believes it to have been authored considerably after Kumārajīva's death and therefore of dubious authenticity.[47]

Next on the list of Heart Sutra translations, in terms of verifiable antiquity, is the translation ascribed to Xuanzang. For most Buddhists today it is the "gold standard" of Heart Sutra translations. This is the version I have on the wall of my home.

Xuanzang is one of the world's best known translators today, with superstar, even quasi-superhero status in much of Asia. And this is not just because of his translation of the Heart Sutra or the lengths he went to obtain Buddhist texts from India, but also because of the hurdles he had to overcome to translate them. Like Kumārajīva, he worked in an age with almost no dictionaries (or computers or internet or databases or Google Translate or artificial intelligence or copy machines or mass production technologies). And in Xuanzang's era, different cultures and languages and writing systems existed in far more isolation than they do today, meaning that bridging arcane Sanskrit and Chinese concepts—moving from a phonetic system to one based on ideograms—required herculean intellectual effort and talent.

Given how long ago Xuanzang lived, there is an extraordinary amount of information about him. He was born in 602 in Chenliu, in Henan Province in China—historically the center of much of Chinese civilization—and he died in 664 in Yufa monastery near Chang-an, the ancient capital now known as Xi'an. China is often thought of today as a huge, unified entity, but it can be seen historically as a culture that has periodically been reconstituted, with dynasties regularly collapsing and invaders taking over and being absorbed (one constant glue being the Chinese writing system). While Xuanzang was still a teenager the Sui dynasty fell apart and—after a period of anarchy—in 618 the Tang dynasty began. The first Tang emperor did not last long. Then, the second emperor, Taizong (626–49), assumed the throne after murdering two of his brothers. He (at least for a while) worked hard to promote Buddhism, and, in the process, presided over a flourishing of culture—the start of what would become a golden age for ancient China.

At an early age, during all the dynastic turmoil, Xuanzang was obsessed with learning about Buddhism and wanted to become a monk. He was ordained at twenty and quickly made a name for himself as an erudite scholar and skilled preacher. But no matter how much he studied scriptures and commentaries at various monasteries, he wanted to know more. And he became increasingly frustrated by the teachings he received, for he saw contradictions and inconsistencies and translation errors in the scriptures and in the Buddhism then practiced in China. As he would write in a report later,

> Though the Buddha was born in the West his Dharma has spread to the East. In the course of translation mistakes may have crept into the texts, and idioms may have been misapplied. When the words are wrong the meaning is lost, and when a phrase is mistaken the doctrine becomes distorted. Hence the saying, "It is necessary to use correct names." What is valuable is the absence of faults![48]

Given that Buddhism had been brought from far away India by missionaries, then translated and absorbed into Chinese in a haphazard way—often indirectly via different languages and intermediary cultures in Central Asia—these inconsistencies were inevitable. But Xuanzang was determined. The Himalayas made going directly south to India nigh impossible, so he resolved to travel west, through the areas many Indian missionaries had first come on their roundabout way to China, and thus make his way to the land of Buddha's birth, where he hoped he could learn about Buddhism at its source. He is reported to have said,

> "I venture to say that under a tree where music has been performed, there must be echoes of the bell and chime stone, and in the five regions of India, the meanings of the ancient texts must be preserved."[49]

In an era when most people probably lived and died in a fifty-mile radius of their birth, this was a truly stupefying resolution, made all the more difficult because Tang emperor Taizong had forbidden common people from traveling to other lands—and especially to the dangerous and wild lands of the Turkic "western tribes" and innumerable enemies.

In 629, at the age of twenty-six, Xuanzang took off on his extraordinary journey. He left the then-capital of Chang'an and—traveling on the Silk Road used by traders—journeyed along the Hexi corridor to Liangzhou (today's Wuwei), a key point on the way to the wilder "Western Regions." His reputation preceded him as he traveled, often ensuring him a warm welcome, but at Liangzhou the governor had been ordered not to let him go further. Nonetheless, with secret help from some allies he continued, traveling at night and resting in the day, despite a warrant out for his arrest. He was entering treacherous territory, as the Silk Road would then pass through a series of oasis towns, with the Gobi desert to the east and the forbidding Taklamakan desert to the west. Traveling companions and guides deserted him and one threatened to rob him, horses ran away or died, and authorities tried to stop him. But he continued undaunted, traveling through the last bastions of official Chinese control at fortified Yumen Pass in the Great Wall of China and then the five signal towers on its periphery that stretched into the desert. At one point, going through the desert alone on a trail marked by the skeletons of unlucky travelers before him, he saw what appeared to be an army of several hundred men. According to Xuanzang's official biography, mostly penned in 688 by the monk Huili, they were

... dressed in furs or coarse cloth, and their camels and horses, as well as banners, flags, and spears, kept on changing their shapes, but gradually disappeared as they approached. At first sight, the Master thought them to be bandits, but as they faded away when they came nearer, he realized that they were bogies and demons.[50]

Xuanzang was entering the Gashun Gobi desert, or what the ancients described as a "desert river," where there was "no bird flying above, nor any beast roaming below; neither was there any water or grass," and he had "only his lonely shadow travelling with him." Buddhism was then in ascendancy in China, and there was also a cult of the Goddess of Mercy, or Avalokiteśvara, so it is not surprising, perhaps, that he would chant the name of the Bodhisattva to protect himself. In what has puzzled some scholars, however, he is also said to have been reciting the *Prajñāpāramitā Hṛdaya Sūtra*—the Heart Sutra—which he is believed to have learned previously in "the region of the Shu," or modern Sichuan, China. There, he had seen a "sick man suffering from a foul skin ulcer and dressed in rags" (in other sources listed as a monk) and given him money for clothes and food. In exchange, the man had taught him the Heart Sutra.

According to Huili, in the desert Xuanzang

... met various evil spirits with strange appearances that surrounded him and refused to be dispelled completely, although he repeated the name of Avalokiteśvara Bodhisattva. But as soon as he uttered

this sutra, all of them disappeared immediately. It
was by depending upon this sutra that he was saved
from many a peril.[51]

For scholars, this passage in Xuanzang's biography raises
several difficult questions that are not easily answered today.
Was he merely taught the mantra portion of the Heart Sutra by
the sick man? It seems unlikely that he would have learned a
Sanskrit version from a monk in Chinese territory, so he presumably learned something in Chinese. But was it an earlier,
existing Chinese translation of the sutra, and if so, which one?
Is there an *ur*-version of the sutra that has never been found?

Be that as it may, Xuanzang somehow survived demons
and daunting deserts, and then had a stroke of good luck when,
again, he found his reputation had preceded him. The king of
quasi-independent Gaochang, Qu Wentai, ruled over an oasis
area near today's Turpan in Xinjiang Province. He was a devout
Buddhist of Chinese extraction who was also allied with the
vast Western Turkic Khaganate. He had already heard of Xuanzang but, far from helping him on his journey to India, des-
perately wanted him to give up his idea and to stay in his own
kingdom forever and teach his subjects. He alternated between
enticements and threats and temporary imprisonment, but,
impressed by Xuanzang's unshakable determination, he eventually relented. He provided Xuanzang with enough gold and
silver and silk as funds to last twenty years, clothes, servants
and attendants, thirty horses, and twenty-five carriers. Most
important, he gave Xuanzang twenty-four letters of introduction to the rulers of other lands further west on his way to India,
including the powerful Turkish Khan, to secure his safe passage.

Ruins of Gaochang, with modern mosque in background.

Today, Gaochang is a major tourist destination in modern China's Xinjiang Province, officially part of the Xinjiang Uyghur Autonomous Region. As the name implies, it is an area that is home to far more than just Han Chinese, having a majority population of now-Muslim Turkic Uyghurs. And as a key junction on the ancient northern Silk Road, connecting Asia all the way to Europe, the region has long been traveled (and lived in) by a remarkably diverse group of people from India, Asia, Central Asia, the Middle East, and even Europe, with different languages, cultures, and religious beliefs—not just Buddhists but also Nestorian Christians, Zoroastrians, Taoists, Confucians, Manicheans, Muslims, Jews, and others.

When Xuanzang was there Gaochang sat on the far western edge of the new Tang Empire's sphere of influence, and it was thus a true jumping-off point, from where he would finally and completely leave the Chinese cultural orbit.

When I traveled to Gaochang as a tourist in 2004, my admiration for Xuanzang only intensified. Gaochang is one of many oasis sites on the northern edge of the forbidding Taklamakan desert, in an area with innumerable and daunting physical barriers for lonely travelers in ancient times to overcome—including the red-colored, barren, and often scorching hot "Flaming Mountains" that are themselves part of the vast and towering Tianshan range. Today, the ancient city's sandy ramparts and crumbling ruins are crowded with foreign and domestic tourists, brought in on air-conditioned buses, cruising around in donkey-pulled carts driven by Uyghurs, the Chinese tourists often wearing white cowboy hats to shield themselves from the sun. The entire area is one of lost civilizations, lost languages, lost cultures, and everywhere a sense of the impermanence of anything made by man. I kept thinking of Percy Bysshe Shelley's famous 1817 poem "Ozymandias," about an ancient statue to the eponymous Egyptian Pharoah:

"... Look on my Works, ye Mighty, and despair!
Nothing beside remains. Round the decay
Of that colossal Wreck, boundless and bare
The lone and level sands stretch far away."[52]

I still have a tourist pamphlet titled "The Ancient History of Gaochang." Written in Chinese, English, and Japanese, it gives a brief history of the kingdom and the city ruins. And it notes how, like many oasis towns in Central Asia, it was invaded by multiple conquerors—not only the Tang Chinese of Xuanzang's era but also Genghis Khan and his Mongol armies in the thirteenth century. And of course it also prominently mentions Xuanzang's visit 1,400 years ago.

The same pamphlet highlights the fact that at the end of the nineteenth and the beginning of the twentieth centuries, "explorers from Russia, Germany, Britain and Japan came to rob Gaochang." Part of the "Great Game," conducted by foreign powers vying for supremacy in Central Asia at the time, archaeologists (and spies) explored the area and "appropriated" many Buddhist and other art objects and texts to take home to museums in their own countries. Like the beautiful and ancient Greek marble statuary in the British Museum—appropriated from the Parthenon in Athens at the beginning of the nineteenth century by Lord Elgin—in China today the "robbing" of "Chinese art" by foreigners is passionately resented and nearly always stressed to tourists. It is a completely understandable emotion, but as far as Buddhist art is concerned, I have always marveled at how much destruction has also been done by non-Europeans.

In truth, Buddhism has not always fared well in China, especially in the Xinjiang area. Depending on the dynasty, there have been attempts to eradicate Buddhism, with thousands of temples and monasteries and manuscripts destroyed. During the Mao Zedong–led Cultural Revolution that began in 1967, vast numbers of temples and monasteries throughout China met the same fate. During Xuanzang's visit to Gaochang, he must have visited the Bezeklik Thousand Buddha Caves, less than a three-hour hike away. In his time, some of these caves, carved into the steep rock walls of cliffs in western Mutou Valley, under the Flaming Mountains, would have contained spectacular Buddhist artwork. Today, despite being a popular tourist attraction, much of the artwork is gone, looted not only by Europeans but also locals. Like much Buddhist art in the now-majority Muslim area, the surviving Buddha and Bodhisattva portraits are usually eyeless, or faceless, vandalized over the centuries by those who regard their images as offensive (or sometimes salable).

TO INDIA AND BACK

After leaving Gaochang, Xuanzang continued on his quest to visit the land of the Buddha. With his letters of introduction, and his reputation as a holy man, he often traveled like royalty, in large caravans of two-humped Bactrian camels and horses and scores of attendants and escorts and considerable funds. But at other times, when robbers or pirates attacked, he escaped with only his life. He traveled through many kingdoms in Central Asia and, while avoiding the Himalayas, crossed the Tianshan, the Pamir, and the Hindukush mountain ranges and made his way to India through Afghanistan and today's Pakistan.

As Sally Wriggins has documented in *The Silk Road Journey of Xuanzang* (2004), it is one of the most extraordinary journeys ever made by an individual, a total of nearly ten thousand miles. It was also so well recorded by Xuanzang, and later by his contemporary biographer, Huili, that his observations have been used by archaeologists to rediscover old ruins in Central Asia. They have also been used by religious scholars to help reconstruct the history of Buddhism in Central Asia and on the Indian subcontinent over 1,400 years ago. Xuanzang even provided us with what may be the first written description of the giant Bamiyan Buddha statues in Afghanistan, a wonder of the world destroyed by the Taliban in 2001. On a far more prosaic and personal level, it's hard for me not to feel awe that he survived his journey. In my own life, 1,400 years after Xuanzang, I have known many otherwise healthy travelers in modern China and India who have been felled by disease, despite water filters and modern immunizations and critical aids such as Cipro and Flagyl. Yet Xuanzang somehow managed to live over sixty years, to what was in his time a ripe old age.

In Huili's account of Xuanzang there are no more direct references to the Heart Sutra after his success in repelling demons in the Gashun Gobi desert, while still on the northern Silk Road. But we can easily deduce in his story that Xuanzang was constantly refining his knowledge of the principles described in the sutra, for he was a devoted Mahayana believer, and in many kingdoms he passed through he was asked to lecture and debate the finer points of various Buddhist sutras, doctrines, and theories. In the kingdom of Kucha, on the far western edge of today's China, the king was not of Chinese descent— surviving images indicate that he had light hair and blue eyes. But he, too, was a devout Buddhist, and his kingdom had "over one hundred monasteries with some five thousand monks who study the Sarvāstivāda school of the Hinayana [pre-Mahayana] teachings." Culturally, Kucha was a bridge to India, with a writing system resembling Sanskrit. One of the venerated sages with whom Xuanzang debated scripture in the kingdom had traveled to India and spent twenty years there.[53] And Kucha had also been the home of the other famous translator of sutras—the previously mentioned Kumārajīva. Nearly two hundred and fifty years before Xuanzang, Kumārajīva had translated many famous sutras into Chinese—including the Diamond and Lotus sutras and, it was long believed (until recently), the Heart Sutra itself.

In 629 Xuanzang crossed the Hindukush Mountains and spent around two years studying scriptures and commentaries at monasteries in Kashmir. From there he entered India proper, where he would spend many more years. He visited monasteries and famous sites related to the historical Buddha, absorbing as much knowledge as he could about various schools of Buddhism, both Mahayana and pre-Mahayana. The diversity of religious sects in the Buddha's homeland must have surprised him, but he never stopped seeking what he believed to be the truth of the Buddha's teachings by studying, debating, and lecturing to others.

Xuanzang visited the sacred Buddhist sites in the Buddhist "Holy Land," such as Lumbini, where the Buddha was born; Bodh Gaya, where Buddha reached enlightenment under what came to be called the Bodhi Tree; Sarnath, where Buddha gave his first sermon; and Kusinagara, where he died. He saw Vulture Peak, where Buddha is said to have given many of his most famous talks, including about the Prajñāpāramitā or Perfection of Wisdom sutras on which the Heart Sutra is based, and where, in the Heart Sutra, Avalokiteśvara lectures Śāriputra, Buddha's favorite disciple. Xuanzang also visited stupas built to contain relics of Śāriputra and to commemorate where he had been born and achieved sainthood.

After three years of travel, Xuanzang spent more time at Nālandā, near Bodh Gaya, than anywhere else. Nālandā was then the most famous Buddhist monastery in the world, with monks coming to study from kingdoms all over, a place of learning so big that Xuanzang's seventh-century biographer, Huili, says (perhaps exaggerating only slightly) that "it had ten thousand host and guest monks" supported by local villagers so they didn't have to beg and could concentrate on their studies. Here again Xuanzang was treated like royalty. Huili describes in detail the luxurious rations Xuanzang was provided, adding, "He had a servant and a Brahman to serve him and was exempted from monastic duties; and when he went out he had an elephant to carry him."[54]

There is no explicit mention of the Heart Sutra during this period in the report Xuanzang later prepared for the Tang emperor, or in Huili's biography. But at the beginning of the twentieth century a version of the Heart Sutra attributed to Xuanzang was discovered at the Buddhist grottos in Dunhuang, with a Sanskrit preface said to be by Amoghavajra (705–74), a monk who, nearly one hundred years after Xuanzang, traveled from China to India and also returned with many important Buddhist texts that he translated. The preface notes that Xuanzang not only used the sutra in the deserts to protect himself, but that if he recited it forty-nine times a magical apparition would appear and help him. At Nālandā, according to the same preface, Xuanzang met the same monk who had first taught him the sutra many years ago in China, a man once terribly sick and old but now young and healthy and actually the Bodhisattva Avalokiteśvara—the implication being that the Bodhisattva had manifested him/herself to Xuanzang to encourage him and protect him on his bold adventure to India, even to inspire him to go there. This account is regarded as being of somewhat dubious provenance by Heart Sutra scholar Harada Wasō, but either way, as Dan Lusthaus notes, "The *Heart Sūtra* became [Xuanzang's] secret weapon, his talismanic amulet, his magical companion, and the facilitator of the epic journey from China to India and back again, for which he has, ever since, been rightfully celebrated."[55]

In Nālandā, Xuanzang also acquired the translation skills for which he would become famous, since he studied not only Buddhist texts but the language in which most were written— Sanskrit. As one of his disciples would comment after his death,

> The Master is dexterously conversant with the Sanskrit language, with which he praised the profound Buddhist texts. He reads Sanskrit books as if they were his own compositions and his intonation still echoes in the air. Strictly adhering to the Buddha's meanings, he does not add any embellishments to his translations. Unknown dialects and previously untranslated Sanskrit terms have been carefully studied and weighed through research and mutual collation with passages from classical Buddhist texts, lest deviations should occur.[56]

In 644, at the age of forty-three, Xuanzang started his long journey home, sent off with a huge retinue, one that started with armies and monks and servants and vast amounts of silver and gold coins and letters of recommendation and horses and an elephant for him to ride. But for Xuanzang, by far the most important thing was the 657 Sanskrit sutras and texts, both Mahayana and pre-Mayahana, and relics and Buddhist ephemera that he had collected. Even with the assistance it would not be an easy journey, since he would retrace some but not all of his trip to India, losing his elephant and crossing mountains ranges and rivers and deserts where, according to biographer Huili, "wayfarers had to look for human and animal skeletons as road signs when they travelled to and fro."[57]

Instead of the Northern Silk Road, on his return Xuanzang took the southern route, which skirted the southern edge of the Taklamakan desert. This was essentially the same route that the famous European Marco Polo is said to have taken in 1271, over six hundred years later. It also took Xuanzang through Dunhuang, a strategic crossroads on the Silk Road, famous for its Buddhist community (and especially its cave paintings and temples), which he had bypassed on his way out. He had already written the Tang emperor, abjectly apologizing for having left the empire so many years earlier, without permission, and explaining his motives. Here, he wrote him again.

In the spring of 645, after a nearly seventeen-year absence, Xuanzang finally arrived with his retinue in the Tang China capital, Chang'an. He was greeted like a conquering hero and surrounded by huge crowds. The next day a formal procession was organized, and both ordinary people and clergy could view a display of tiny relics of the Buddha's bones and seven small statutes of the Buddha, of both gold and sandalwood. Most important, bound in 520 bundles and carried by twenty horses, Xuanzang had 657 Buddhist texts, mainly of the Mahayana school, and even texts on Indian logic and grammar, written on palm leaves.

Soon after Xuanzang met Emperor Taizong, he again apologized for leaving China without permission. He was forgiven his transgressions and later ordered to create a detailed report of his trip, with as much information as possible on the lands that he had seen, today famously known as his *Great Tang Record of the Western Regions*. Even more important, the emperor gave Xuanzang everything he needed to assemble a team of learned experts to help him translate into Chinese the huge number of sutras and texts he had brought back. The emperor ensured that copies would be made of each one and distributed, so that "all the people in the whole land might receive the doctrines that they had not heard before." And he even composed a flowery preface to be placed at the beginning of many of them, extolling both Xuanzang and the teachings of Buddha. On top of that, he had a special monastery created, the Great Ci'en, where Xuanzang and his team could translate and his texts and treasures be housed. And when the emperor Taizong passed away and his son Gaozong ascended the throne, Xuanzang continued to receive all sorts of favors from the new emperor, including a special pagoda to house the most valuable treasures.[58]

Xuanzang would continue translating for nearly twenty more years, working ceaselessly at various monasteries. He was obviously a perfectionist, and unlike his famous predecessor, the monk Kumārajīva, who was famous for eliminating repetitiveness in Indian sutras and rendering them in easier to understand Chinese, Xuanzang was a stickler for accuracy—to the point that he has also been described as someone known for his "awkward phraseology."[59] But he could sometimes translate texts into elegant and refined Chinese, as was the case with his version of the Heart Sutra, which has become the "gold standard" in China.

Exactly how and when the Xuanzang translation of the Heart Sutra was done is shrouded in historical mist. According to Xuanzang's contemporary biographers, Huili and Yancong, at the end of 656 the new emperor and his wife (the later-to-be-notorious Empress Wu Zetian) had a son, who they agreed could enter monkhood and who Xuanzang hoped would become his disciple. A month later, in a letter, an overjoyed Xuanzang referred to presents made to the baby of a special religious robe, items that acolytes might need, including rosaries and incense burners and a copy of what in English translation is referred to as the Prajñāpāramitā or "Perfection of Wisdom" sutras—the thoughts of which the Heart Sutra is said to exemplify—"written in golden characters in one fascicle and kept in a case."[60]

From this description, it is logical to assume that the sutra referred to here was actually a copy of the Heart Sutra. After all, according to his biographer, Xuanzang and his team did not begin to translate the magisterial *Mahāprajñāpāramitā*—a huge compilation of Prajñāpāramitā literature said to be six hundred rolls in the Chinese translation—until 660, not completing it until 663. And the sheer immensity of the entire compilation would have made it impossible to present it as one fascicle in a case. Indeed, Huili's original Chinese text specifically identifies this as the "Heart Sutra." Dating of Xuanzang's first translation of the Heart Sutra varies, but according to the *Korean Buddhist Canon*, a catalog of Buddhist works in Chinese (derived from a collection from the thirteenth century, stored in a monastery in South Korea), Xuanzang had already translated it in just one day, on July 8, 649, at the Cui Wei palace, in the Zhongnan Mountains.[61]

Xuanzang's body finally gave out on February 5, 664. Before he expired, he is said to have murmured the following to his disciples:

> "The aggregate of matter is void; and the aggregates of perception, conception, volition, and consciousness are also void. The realm of sight is void; and [all sense realms] up to the realm of mind are also void. The realm of sight-perception is void; and [all sense-perception realms] up to the realm of the mental faculty are also void. Ignorance is void; and [all *nidānas*] up to old age and death are also void. Even enlightenment is void; and voidness itself is also void."[62]

As Dan Lusthaus, a Buddhist scholar in the United States has noted, allowing for differences that might arise in the English translation of Huili's biography, or the fact that it may have been rendered very loosely by the original author/s, it sounds surprisingly like the initial expository section of the Heart Sutra.[63]

TRIPIṬAKA MASTER AND HIS TRANSLATION

If, in his lifetime, Xuanzang was regarded as a hero, after death his fame would propel him into heavenly heights, for he would be elevated to the status of saint and eventually become a mythological superhero. He became known as the "Tripiṭaka Master," or the master of the "three baskets," the Buddhist canon.

In Xi'an, the Giant Wild Goose Pagoda was built to house Xuanzang's treasures and relics, and it remains a hugely

Temple stamp from Hōryū-ji in Japan, with a popular depiction of the traveling Xuanzang. Bold characters say "Not East," symbolizing his resolve to never deviate a step from his quest to reach India, in the "West."

popular tourist attraction. Reliquaries or stupas believed to contain some fragments of Xuanzang are not only in China proper, but also in Taiwan and even Japan. And there are images and statues of Xuanzang, often showing him as a traveling mendicant monk with a staff. Sometimes, as in Yakushi-ji temple in Nara, Japan, he is shown seated, brush in one hand, and palm-leaf Sanskrit sutras in another. But most often he is shown lugging a giant box-like backpack (laden with palm-leaf Sanskrit sutras from India) with a large woven hat-like structure on top providing shade in the desert heat, an incense burner dangling in the front. He has sandals on his feet, a necklace of skulls, a sword at his waist, a horse-hair flapper in his right hand, and a sutra in his left. This is the type of statue that adorns some temples in China, Taiwan, and Japan and stands in front of the Xuanzang Memorial Hall at Nālandā in modern India, with the English inscription "Xuan Zang belongs to a galaxy of world Citizens whose great mission was to interpret, for the good of mankind, sublime values of human civilization."

Of course, during much of his return from India Xuanzang was actually riding on an elephant and guarded by scores of soldiers, porters, and attendants, but that is harder to depict in statuary. In more modern media, the historical Xuanzang is lauded in East Asia in books and documentaries. In 2016, even one big budget live-action feature film, appropriately titled *Xuanzang*, was shot in both China and India. One of the theme songs was a musical version of the Heart Sutra, sung by the popular Faye Wong.

While other translations of the Heart Sutra have been done over the centuries, unless they are a Tibetan or Sanskrit "long recension" almost all copies in use around the world today are ultimately based on the Chinese translation attributed to Xuanzang. To demonstrate "authenticity," sometimes copies in Asia even have his name on them as the translator, often rendered as 唐三藏法師玄奘譯 ("Translation by the Tang Tripiṭaka Master Xuanzang").

Many mysteries surround the Chinese version of the Heart Sutra attributed to Xuanzang, but some new evidence has recently come to light. On September 24, 2016, Chinese media reported the discovery of a stone carving of a copy of Xuanzang's translation at the Yunchun temple in Fangshan, a rural area near Beijing. In the two or three centuries before Xuanzang was born, China had undergone one of its occasional periods of political and social turmoil and disunion, until reunited by the short-lived Sui dynasty (581–618), which in turn created the foundation for the prosperous and cultural flowering of the Tang dynasty of Xuanzang's era. Even though Buddhism continued to spread throughout China in this period, during the turmoil there were attempts made to suppress and even eradicate it (as there would be later, over and over again).

The Buddhist monks of Yunchun, painfully aware of political instability and showing extraordinary prescience, decided that the best way to preserve the teachings of the Buddha for future generations would be to carve them in stone slabs, called "stele," which would then be stored in caves in the hills. Thousands of these slabs were thus carved over the centuries, and in 2016 experts discovered that one of them, stored in Cave 8, was indeed the Heart Sutra. Moreover, and more remarkably, it had inscribed on it the fact that it had been translated by none other than Xuanzang, at the direction of the then-emperor, and carved in stone in 661. In China and Japan this was big news, but elsewhere, other than a detailed 2019 published paper by Jayarava Attwood, this find attracted surprisingly little attention among academic researchers around the world. Yet since Xuanzang's paper versions have vanished, if carved in 661 these stones may currently be the oldest known copy of a translation of the Heart Sutra attributed to him, done three years before his death in 664.[64]

Because of the Heart Sutra's brevity and the quasi-magical power it was believed to hold, copying Xuanzang's version of it became a way not only to spread the word of Mahayana Buddhism but also to accrue personal merit and protection. Aiding the sutra's popularity was its brevity, which made it well suited for chanting and calligraphic copying and for large and small wall-hangings and carvings in temples and other sites. And this is still the case throughout Mahayana regions of East Asia.

In Taiwan, Buddhism remains strong and outside the influences of Communism and the Cultural Revolution. Outside the southern city of Kaohsiung, the Fo Guang Shan Monastery has created what might be called an enormous Buddhist theme park, with museums and pagodas and historical statuary. There is a statue of Xuanzang, of course, and innumerable references and connections to his version of the Heart Sutra. And in the huge Sutra Library of the monastery an entire, gigantic wall is dramatically inscribed with Xuanzang's version of the Heart Sutra, done in the calligraphic style of the sect's master, Hsing Yun. Elsewhere, in Taipei, another prominent and global Zen sect known as the Dharma Drum Mountain maintains the Nung Chan monastery. There, one entire wall of an enormous, very modern, primarily steel and glass Buddha Hall has a giant cutout of the Heart Sutra, allowing sunlight through each character and creating, as the sect's website said in 2019, "changes with the flow of natural light, reminding us that life's conditions are impermanent, forever arising and perishing."[65]

In Hong Kong, one of the more original visual representations of the Heart Sutra is on Lantau Island, near the Po Lin monastery. Called the "Wisdom Path," it was created in 2005 by the late Hong Kong–based Sinologist and artist Professor Rao Zongyi (or Jao Tsung-I in Cantonese). In 1980 Rao had visited Mount Taishang, one of five sacred mountains in mainland China and a World Heritage Site where, nearby, there is a colossal inscription of the Diamond Sutra on an ancient rock riverbed, said to be the largest such inscription in China. Inspired, the professor resolved to create something of similar scale on Lantau Island, using the Heart Sutra, which like the far longer Diamond Sutra, exemplifies the spirit of the Prajñā-pāramitā sutras.

The end result was thirty-eight giant timber columns standing on a hill, each eight to ten meters tall and a meter wide, arrayed on a grand expanse in the same figure-of-eight "infinity" symbol used in mathematics. The timber columns are cut with flat faces to resemble the bamboo slats or "slips" (*zhu jian*) used in ancient China before paper was broadly available, and each one has a short phrase from Xuanzang's Heart Sutra carved into its face, based on calligraphy done by Professor Rao. By following a path below visitors can slowly read the entire sutra in the midst of dramatic scenery. The twenty-third column, or pole, at the top of the hill is left blank, to symbolize the "emptiness" concept of the Heart Sutra.

At the bottom of the hill, a commemorative metal plaque in Chinese, Japanese, and English describes the site's origin and, given the difficulty of the task, courageously attempts to explain the Heart Sutra's meaning:

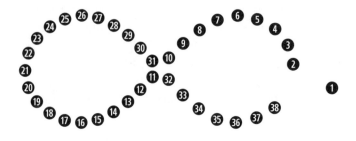

1	*The Heart of the Prajna-Paramita Sutra*	21	through the reliance on Prajna-paramita
2, 3	When Avalokitesvara Bodhisattva is practicing the profound Prajna-paramita	22	Have no attachment and hindrance in their minds.
4	he becomes aware and mindful of the emptiness (nature) of the five skandhas	23	
5	and thus attains deliverance from all suffering. Sariputra,	24	There is no more fear,
6	matter is not different from emptiness, and emptiness is not different from matter.	25	and distant from mistaken views and illusory thinking,
7	Matter is emptiness and emptiness is matter.	26	Ultimately: The Final Nirvana. Buddhas of the past, present, and future
8	So too are sensation, cognition, volition and consciousness.	27	all rely on Prajna-paramita
9	Sariputra, the emptiness character of all phenomena,	28	to attain Annutara-samyak-sambodhi.

10	neither arises nor ceases, is neither pure nor impure,	29	Therefore, know that Prajna-paramita
11	and neither increases nor decreases.	30	is the great wondrous mantra, the great radiant mantra,
12	Therefore, in emptiness: there is no matter,	31	the unsurpassed mantra, and the unequalled mantra.
13	no sensation, cognition, volition or consciousness,	32	It can eradicate all suffering, and it is genuine and not false.
14	no eye, ear, nose, tongue, body, or mind,	33	Therefore, utter the Prajna-paramita mantra—
15	no sight, sound, scent, taste, tangibles, or dharma,	34	Chant:
16	no field of the eye up to no field of mental consciousness,	35	Gate Gate Paragate
17	no ignorance or the ending of ignorance,	36	Parasamgate
18	up to no ageing and death or the ending of ageing and death,	37	Bodhisvaha!
19	no suffering, no cause of suffering, no ending of suffering, and no path, no wisdom and also no attainment.	38	May the whole region be forever blessed with felicitous harmony and prosperity.
20	Because there is nothing obtainable, Bodhisattvas		

English translation © University of Hong Kong, Centre of Buddhist Studies. From a 2018 tourist pamphlet.

"Wisdom Path," Ngong Ping, Lantau Island, Hong Kong. Photograph by Fiammetta Hsu.

The Heart Sutra articulates the doctrine of "emptiness." But this "emptiness" must not be understood as the denial of phenomenal existence—it is not nihilism. What it teaches is that everything is dependently arisen from conditions; an event (a "thing") occurs if and only if the adequacy of conditions obtains. Since everything is dependently arisen, there is no such thing as an eternally abiding entity. The doctrine of emptiness also spells out the relativity of all views. When one acquires this Wisdom of "emptiness," one will realize that all physical and mental events are in a constant process of change, and accordingly everything can be changed by modifying the conditions. Understanding the relativity of all standpoints will also prevent one from becoming irrationally attached to things. In this way, one will come to be free from mental obstructions, and attain to perfect harmony and bliss. At the same time, with the understanding that all are dependently arisen, one will treasure and make good use of the conditions that are available, realizing the idea of benefiting oneself and others.

At the very end, the plaque kindly informs us that one may initially find it difficult to understand the Heart Sutra, "not least because of its unusually profound doctrine. But if one persists with receptivity, reading and meditating on it, one will eventually come to comprehend the secret of the universe and the truth of life contained therein."

5

Monkey

In East Asia, the fame of the historical Xuanzang pales in comparison to that of the *legendary* Xuanzang. I was reminded of this during a visit, in 2017, to a movie theater converted into a museum in Taiwan's old Jiufen mining town. One display had a small box-like picture "viewer" for children, from 1934, that used paper strips with illustrated stories on them. Taiwan was then part of the Japanese Empire, but the workers at the mine were Chinese. There were two paper strips, or stories, on display. One was a Donald Duck story, in Chinese. The other was the story, also in Chinese, of the legendary Xuanzang, shown on a white horse, meeting a monkey.

The story of Xuanzang's journey to India held such popular appeal that over the centuries it morphed into folk legend. Nearly a thousand years later, in the sixteenth century, it was immortalized in a vast and sprawling novel titled *Xiyouji*, or "Journey to the West," attributed to Wu Cheng'en. In the novel, the basic story—that of Xuanzang traveling over vast distances through amazing hardships to India to retrieve Buddhist sutras—was retained. But Xuanzang became a different character, a naïve monk named Tang Sanzang ("Tripiṭaka"), sent by the Tang emperor Taizong from Chang'an. Tang San-zang had more flaws and weaknesses than Xuanzang and a tendency to get into predicaments. Needing help and protection from monsters and demons, in the story Avalokiteśvara (Guanyin) provides him with escort-disciples, some with supernatural powers. These include Sun Wukong, a "Monkey King"; Zhu Bajie, a complicated pig-human; Sha Wujing, a rough-looking ogre-general from heaven; and Yulong, a white horse, formerly a dragon prince. In many ways Sun Wukong had the starring role, so much so that in 1943 the famous British scholar Arthur Waley titled his English translation *Monkey: Folk Novel of China*. Today, nearly all children throughout East Asia know *Journey to the West* because it has also been incorporated and reworked into different modern media, including live-action films, comic books, and animation, in China and especially Japan.

In 1941, the Wan brothers in Japanese-occupied Shanghai made part of the story into China's first animated feature, *Tie shan gongzhu*, or "Princess Iron Fan." After the war, Japanese manga and anime artists helped give the story its vast global momentum. Starting in 1952, inspired by the Wan brothers, Tezuka Osamu, known as Japan's "God of Manga," began serializing *Boku no Songokū* ("My Songokū") as a manga. This was turned into a feature animation titled *Saiyūki* ("Journey to the West") and an animated TV series in 1967 titled *Gokū no Dai-bōken* ("Gokū's Grand Adventure"), and even a sci-fi variant in 1989. In the English world, many young baby boomers got their first exposure to Japanese anime when the feature film was shown as *Alakazam the Great*.

In 1978 Japan also turned the sixteenth-century novel *Journey to the West* into a live-action TV series, shot in China and

San Francisco Chinatown mural, 2018.

Mongolia, creating a huge hit in England, Australia, and other English-speaking countries under the title of *Monkey*. Today's fans may not be aware of it, but the same novel was a primary inspiration for Akira Toriyama's martial-arts-infused *Dragon Ball* manga and anime series, which since 1995 has become a blockbuster, global franchise.[66] Where I live in the San Francisco Bay Area, in 2019 images of the legendary Xuanzang and his "disciples" could be seen in Chinatown murals, at least one showing Zhu Bajie with a tattoo on his stomach saying "Notorious P.I.G.," in a humorous allusion to the rap pioneer Notorious B.I.G., who was murdered in 1997.

Wu Cheng'en's sixteenth-century novel does not ignore the Heart Sutra but instead elevates it above its status in

Huili's seventh-century biography of Xuanzang (discussed in the previous chapter). In the novel, meticulously translated into English with copious notes in four volumes totaling 1,880 pages by Professor Anthony C. Yu of the University of Chicago, Tripiṭaka (Xuanzang) is described as having learned the Heart Sutra from a "Crow's Nest Chan Master" who warned him of all the evils and hardships he would face on his journey to India:

> "But all those *māra* hindrances along the way are hard to dispel. I have a Heart Sūtra here in this scroll; it has fifty-four sentences containing two hundred and seventy characters. When you meet these *māra* hindrances, recite the sūtra and you will not suffer any injury or harm." Tripitaka prostrated himself on the ground and begged to receive it, whereupon the Chan Master imparted the sūtra by reciting it orally.[67]

The novel then includes the full text of the Heart Sutra, which Xuanzang remembers in its entirety after hearing it once. It is of course the Chinese translation attributed to the historical Xuanzang. In the original text of the novel, although the Chan Master mentions 270 characters, when one subtracts titles, etc., the text body is exactly 260 characters long. It is, in other words, the same as the copy I have on my wall at home, minus the two characters (一切) added for emphasis in Japanese versions.

UNEARTHING A COMPLICATED HISTORY

Xuanzang's historical and legendary notoriety has rippled through time, sometimes generating a complicated cause and effect on his legacy and the sutras he so loved. Before the historical Xuanzang arrived back in Chang'an in 645, he wrote the Tang emperor from Dunhuang, famous today for the remote Mogao grottos. These are among the best known and most spectacular of numerous remote Buddhist cave complexes in China, carved into cliffs by impossibly determined Buddhist monks, probably starting in the fourth century. Xuanzang certainly visited them. Known also as the "Caves of a Thousand Buddhas," they contained Buddhist paintings and sculptures and silk banners and repositories for texts. Even today they remain a semi-sacred place for Buddhist pilgrims from around the world, especially Japan and Korea. They are a UNESCO World Heritage Site and a deserved wonder of the world.

At the turn of the nineteenth century, the era's great powers in the world were vying for influence and control in Central Asia. British, German, Hungarian, French, Japanese, and Russian explorers, some archaeologists (including some spies masquerading as archaeologists), and some simple treasure hunters were actively exploring ancient Silk Road sites and lost civilizations in and around the Taklamakan and Gobi deserts. Dunhuang and the Mogao caves were in an oasis at the intersection of the northern and southern Silk Roads, but because of their remoteness the caves had largely escaped exploitation and had largely remained outside of Western knowledge or interest.

As Peter Hopkirk, author of *Foreign Devils on the Silk Road*, has vividly documented, that all changed with the arrival of the Hungarian-born British archaeologist, Aurel Stein. Stein had previously explored many parts of British India, using a French translation of the report Xuanzang made to the Tang emperor Taizong upon his return to Chang'an (Xi'an) in 645. This translation had convinced Stein of the accuracy and

Entrance to the Mogao grottoes in Dunhuang.

usefulness of Xuanzang's work, which he referred to over and over again, phoneticizing Xuanzang's Chinese name as Hiuen-Tsiang. By 1900–1901, when Stein began exploring the desert oases of Central Asia (then under only loose Chinese control during the waning years of the Qing dynasty), he found that "It seemed indeed that in the memory of Chinese Buddhists Hiuen-Tsiang lives like a glorified Arhat or Bodhisattva." Indeed, Stein's knowledge of Xuanzang and his journey, and his esteem for him, proved increasingly useful:

> The historical sense innate in educated Chinese and the legendary knowledge I found to prevail among them of Hiuen-Tsiang, the great Buddhist pilgrim, whom I claimed as my guide and patron saint, certainly helped me in explaining the objects of my explorations to my Chinese friends and enlisting their personal interest.[68]

On a second expedition, conducted between 1906 and 1908 and following roughly on Xuanzang's southern Silk Road trail, Stein was even more convinced that the monk was his true "patron saint." And he put him to even more shameless use.

As early as 1902, Stein had heard about the spectacular "Caves of the Thousand Buddhas" to the southeast of Dunhuang from a friend who had been on an 1879 Hungarian expedition to them. He was determined to visit them. When he finally arrived on March 16, 1907, he was astounded by the number of caves built like honeycombs into precipitous cliffs—and also by the Buddhist art and statuary preserved within them. Stein had heard vague rumors of ancient manuscripts.

And sure enough, he learned that a Taoist priest named Wang Yuanlu had been acting as an unofficial guardian of the caves and, indeed, that a few years previously Wang had accidentally come across a huge cache of ancient manuscripts hidden in one of them. These manuscripts represented one of the world's greatest collections of ancient texts in not only Chinese but a variety of other ancient languages, preserved over a thousand years by the dry and desert climate. Wang had kept them under lock and key and happened to be absent when Stein first arrived.

After exploring briefly in other nearby areas, a determined Stein returned on May 21 and finally met Wang. He found him to be, like himself, a huge admirer of Xuanzang, to the point of building his own temple space and decorating it with wall paintings depicting Xuanzang's journey to India to retrieve sutras. Stein was a relatively enlightened person for his era, but he was unable to suppress a burning desire to not only see the hidden cache of manuscripts, but—if at all possible—take them back to London for further analysis (especially since he couldn't read Chinese). In his mind, he could easily rationalize this. He would not be looting but liberating them from dark and dusty confinement and an uncertain future for modern and systematic study. He knew that it was wrong from the Chinese perspective, but Chinese control in the Dunhuang area was then tenuous at best.

By cleverly advertising and inflating his affinity with Xuanzang, through his interpreter Stein was able to get Wang to show him some samples from the library-cave (now known as "Cave 17"). When these first samples coincidentally proved to be copies of Chinese translations of sutras from India—copies of work apparently done by none other than Xuanzang (whom they also referred to as "T'ang-sêng")—Stein and his interpreter took this as a kind of karmic authorization:

> "Was it not 'T'ang-sêng' himself, ... who at the opportune moment had revealed the hiding-place of that manuscript hoard to an ignorant priest in order to prepare for me, his admirer and disciple from distant India, a fitting antiquarian reward on the westernmost confines of China proper?"[69]

As Stein later gloated in his account, *Ruins of Desert Cathay*, by using this ruse, along with a tiny bribe of "four horse-shoes of silver," or about five hundred Indian rupees, he was eventually able to enlist Wang as a co-conspirator in his plot and gain access to the cave library. It was one of the largest caches of ancient manuscripts ever uncovered, obtained for a pittance, and he was astounded by their excellent condition in the desert clime. Beyond just viewing the material, he was also able to persuade Wang to spend over a week secretly hauling out special selections for him in Chinese and Tibetan and other ancient languages both known and unknown. Cartloads upon cartloads of an estimated thirteen thousand manuscripts and other materials in all were removed, which he would take back to London to deposit in the British Museum. In the process, he would earn the undying enmity of the modern Chinese people, who still regard what he did as yet another brazen looting of national treasures by arrogant imperialist powers when China was at its weakest in the final years of the Qing dynasty (while downplaying the domestic destruction that has also occurred).

The library cave may have originally contained some fifty

thousand medieval scrolls, documents, and silk paintings. Stein unfortunately could not read Chinese, so he was limited in his understanding of what he actually removed (which also included items of dubious value and some forgeries). But he did take away some true treasures, including a ninth-century copy of the Diamond Sutra, considered the world's first dated printed book, and many copies of the Heart Sutra that had been rendered centuries after Xuanzang. Stein would not be the only foreigner to remove documents from the library cave. He was followed a year later by the great French Sinologist Paul Pelliot, who removed even more manuscripts from Cave 17, again with the aid of the same Taoist priest. And Pelliot was followed by Russians, Japanese, and Americans, with the result that the contents of Cave 17, and many other sites, are today scattered among institutions around the world, making the job of researchers exceedingly difficult.[70]

In 1994 the International Dunhuang Project launched, with the goal of coordinating research and eventually making as many materials as possible viewable online and searchable, in effect crowd-sourcing research into what remains an often unexplored past. It is a vast undertaking, requiring decades of laborious work, scrutinizing and cataloging ancient documents from over twenty languages and scripts (including ancient Chinese, Sanskrit, Sogdian, Tibetan, Runic-Turki, Uyghur, Hebrew, and even unknown languages) and then trying to translate them into their modern, more universal equivalents. The end result will be a better understanding of how Buddhism was transmitted from India to China throughout Central Asia, of ancient languages and their pronunciation, and of the culture of the ancient Silk Road. And it will further our understanding of the Heart Sutra and its evolution.

觀自在菩薩行深般若波羅蜜多時照見五蘊皆空度一切苦厄舍利子色不異空空不異色色即是空空即是色受想行識亦復如是舍利子是諸法空相不生不滅不垢不淨不增不減是故空中無色無受想行識無眼耳鼻舌身意無色聲香味觸法無眼界乃至無意識界無無明亦無無明盡乃至無老死亦無老死盡無苦集滅道無智亦無得以無所得故菩提薩埵依般若波羅蜜多故心無罣礙無罣礙故無有恐怖遠離顛倒夢想究竟涅槃三世諸佛依般若波羅蜜多故得阿耨多羅三藐三菩提故知般若波羅蜜多是大神咒是大明咒是無上咒是無等等咒能除一切苦真實不虛故說般若波羅蜜多咒即說咒曰揭諦揭諦波羅揭諦波羅僧揭諦菩提薩婆訶

Many different copies of the Heart Sutra have emerged from Cave 17, from different eras and languages, making intertextual and interlingual research far easier than before. One of the most extraordinary copies "appropriated" by Aurel Stein from Cave 17 is currently in the British Library. It is sometimes reproduced in books and other places. One copy currently graces the library wall in the Dharma Drum Mountain monastery and college complex outside of Taipei, in Taiwan. Apparently created in the ninth or tenth century, long after Xuanzang had passed away, the 260 characters of this Chinese Xuanzang "translation" are arranged on paper 47 x 22 cm in size, in an intricate matrix in the shape of a pagoda. The characters forming the spire of the pagoda, when read vertically down, clearly are the title of the Heart Sutra. Yet the rest of the characters, while all taken from the Heart Sutra, at first glance do not appear to be arranged in any logical order at all and are merely arrayed to create the image of a pagoda. Nonetheless, if one looks carefully, tiny lines can be seen to connect the characters, subtly telling the reader the correct sequence to read them. When the lines are followed and the characters are read in proper order, the entire sutra—and its mantra—come alive. To understand the genius involved in this concept, it would be rather like constructing an outline image of the United States Congress out of all 272 words in Abraham Lincoln's Gettysburg Address in no apparent order, with faint lines connecting the words like a map, showing diligent readers, willing to follow the words in the correct sequence, that what they are really looking at is not a building at all, but something with a profoundly moving message.

< Copy of ninth- to tenth-century Heart Sutra scroll from Mogao caves. Courtesy of British Library.

6

An American Thesis

With the history and legend of Xuanzang so firmly embedded in East Asian cultures, it was perhaps inevitable that Jan Nattier's seventy-one-page 1992 academic paper "The Heart Sūtra: A Chinese Apocryphal Text?" would create controversy. This was particularly so in Japan, where until recently most of the academic writing and research on the Heart Sutra has been done. As Nattier told me when I was writing this book,

> It was around 1989, and I was teaching about the Prajñāpāramitā Sutras for the first time to students at the University of Hawaii. The paper that I wrote on the Heart Sutra came about completely by accident. Specifically, it was triggered by what happened when I was teaching my students about the Large Sutra and the Heart Sutra in the Prajñāpāramitā texts. One night, I was studying both the Sanskrit and Chinese versions of the Large Sutra [the *Pañcaviṃśatisāhasrikā Prajñāpāramitā*, or Perfection of Wisdom in Twenty-five Thousand Lines] and the Heart Sutra, and I noticed for the first time that the core section of the

Heart Sutra was in both sutras, and that in the two
Chinese texts the wording matched almost exactly.
But in the Sanskrit versions of both sutras, though
the content was the same, the wording was completely different. In other words, the Chinese texts
aligned, but the Sanskrit texts did not.[71]

A specialist in Mahayana Buddhism, Nattier had studied
comparative religion and completed her doctorate at Harvard
under the Committee on Inner Asian and Altaic Studies, which
fits thematically into studies of Buddhism and its transmission
into China along the ancient Silk Road. She also had expertise
in a broad range of languages, including Sanskrit, Chinese,
Japanese, classical Mongolian, and Tibetan. She had started
her career studying Mongolian, where sutras were translated
mainly from Tibetan texts but also included terms in Uyghur,
some of which had been "transcribed" rather than translated.
As she says,

Because of this experience, when I looked carefully
at the Chinese and Sanskrit texts I knew immediately that the Sanskrit version of the Heart Sutra
was a back-translation [from Chinese].... I had never
planned to do work on the Heart Sutra at all. But
I instantly knew what had happened. I was totally
stunned! I had never imagined anything like this, and
I certainly hadn't gone looking for it.[72]

For her 1992 paper, Nattier compared different versions
of the Heart Sutra in different languages and translations, and

came to the conclusion that the Heart Sutra was probably not, as was widely believed, translated by Xuanzang from a Sanskrit original that represented the spoken word of Buddha. Instead, it was more likely to be what is called in the West "apocryphal" text. In other words, and in this case, that it had been compiled or edited or translated from other material within China by Xuanzang or his team of translators, and that it was not based on an original Sanskrit text that he had brought from India.

Nattier's paper appeared in the *Journal of the International Association of Buddhist Studies* two years before the founding of the International Dunhuang Project, which would eventually make it so much easier to do online intertextual and interlingual comparisons of the sutra. But even then, she was hardly the first scholar to question the provenance of a Buddhist sutra.

In common parlance, "apocryphal," at least as I understand it, has two meanings, one being something of unsure authenticity, the other being something "hidden" or "secret." In the Christian world, where the word has a long and unique history, some early scriptures and writings, treasured but of dubious provenance (but nonetheless perhaps having value), are incorporated into the Catholic and Episcopalian Bibles as "Apocrypha" and left out of most Protestant Bibles or added as an "Addendum." It's probably why a Holy Bible given to me when I was ten—the 1952 Revised Standard Edition—does not contain them. (The preface to it hints at the controversy accompanying any changes to the Bible over the centuries, noting that in 1536 William Tyndale "was publicly executed and burned at the stake" for creating the first English translation directly from the original Hebrew and Greek scriptures.)[73]

In the Buddhist world there are of course also texts of dubious authenticity or lineage, and in both China and Japan a variety of words have been used to describe them. In Japan, where scholars such as Mochizuki Shinkō (1869–1948) were studying such texts nearly fifty years before Nattier's paper, they have often been referred to as 偽経 and 疑経. Both words are pronounced exactly the same (*gikyō*), but the first character of the former has a strong connotation of "false" or "forged" sutras, whereas the first character of the latter implies "doubtful." When described in English as "apocryphal" sutras—a word so fraught with meaning from the Christian world, with its long history of bloody disagreements—problems can obviously occur, especially because Buddhist sutras exist in a completely different cultural context.

At the University of California, in Berkeley, "Buddhist apocryphal studies" was already a field of study in 1982, and in 1990 it resulted in a collection of scholarly essays titled *Chinese Buddhist Apocrypha*, edited by Robert E. Buswell, Jr.

In his introduction, Buswell wrote that in Buddhist traditions formed outside of India it is "sacrosanct" that their scriptures be translated from works from India, usually from Sanskrit, into their own languages. Often, the scriptures even have statements attached, indicating the translator's name, the date of the translation, and the location, to establish authenticity. While noting the problems that have emerged in Buddhism over scriptural "authenticity," he also alludes to the dilemma scholars have faced in using Western terms like "apocryphal."

It now appears that many Buddhist scriptures were
not "translations" at all, but were composed within
the indigenous cultures of Asia and in the native languages of those regions. It is to such scriptures that
the term "Buddhist apocrypha" is meant to refer.[74]

Recognizing the occasionally pejorative connotation of
the term "apocrypha," Buswell was careful to note that, were
it not for their unwieldiness, it might have been better to
use the terms "indigenous scriptures" or "original [Chinese]
scriptures" instead. Going a step further, he noted that not
just Chinese Buddhist scriptures but "in a very real sense, all
Mahayana Sutras ... are "apocryphal."

Modern scholars know, for example, that most
Mahayana scriptures were certainly composed after
the Buddha's time and represent stages in the adap-
tation of Buddhism to contemporary social situations
and philosophical developments in India.[75]

A DISRUPTIVE PERSPECTIVE

Jan Nattier's approach generated so much attention in Japan
not just for her methodology and the remarkable conclusions
she had reached. It was also because she had concentrated
on one of the most beloved sutras or texts in the Mahayana
world—the Heart Sutra—and had used the word "apocryphal"
in the title of her paper (which, as we shall see, in Japan was
later translated as 偽経, with its connotations of "forgery").
As she wrote, the sutra is "one of the most familiar pieces of

Buddhist writing both in traditional Mahayana Buddhist societies and in modern academic circles. Yet it may be our very familiarity with this scripture that has inhibited our ability to gain a clear picture of its ancestry."[76]

Most mass-market books about the Heart Sutra, both in the West and especially in Asia, try in some way to explain its meaning. And many of these books are of a doctrinal nature, often produced by practitioners of various Buddhist sects who have an agenda. As a result, any objective study questioning the inherent assumed nature or origins of the sutra is liable to collide at some point with the world of faith. In any religion, radical new interpretations or translations of ancient scriptures are often resisted—although arguably less in the world of Buddhism than in Abrahamic and monotheistic religions, with their more monolithic, centralized traditions.

Academics and researchers themselves form another community with an investment in the Heart Sutra. For most of the twentieth century, serious scholars from around the world have painstakingly tried to reconstruct or deduce what a long-lost original *ur*-text (in Sanskrit) of the Heart Sutra might have looked like, using Sanskrit copies created long after Xuanzang's time or even translations from Sanskrit into Tibetan and other languages. Finding the Sanskrit *ur*-text has been a long-cherished goal, but if Nattier is right and there never was one, much of the work of these scholars may have been largely for naught.

Four years before Nattier's paper was published in 1992, her husband, the late and renowned Buddhologist John McRae, had written a paper in the same journal about Chinese Chan (Zen) commentaries on the Heart Sutra. In it he had foreshadowed many of her conclusions about its authenticity and origins, boldly stating in his first line that "The *Prajñā-pāramitā Hṛdaya* is a Chinese text." But he was careful to note in the next sentence: "True, the words themselves were translated from an Indian original, and there do exist Sanskrit manuscripts to establish this authentic South Asian pedigree."[77]

Nattier's real contribution in her paper was to be able to step back and look at the big picture of the sutra's evolution, skillfully dissecting its contradictions. If a translation, why was the sutra, especially the short version (which appeared long before the slightly "longer" version popular in Tibet and in India), not following the normal conventions of most Indian Sanskrit or even Mahayana and especially Prajñāpāramitā sutras? Why was it missing the normal framework of sutras, which start out with "Thus have I heard" and specifically mention the Buddha (not just Avalokiteśvara) speaking at a specific location (such as Vulture Peak, which is not mentioned in the short version)? Why was Avalokiteśvara, and not Buddha, speaking to Buddha's disciple, Śāriputra? Why was Śāriputra depicted as the listener and not disciples more commonly used in other sutras, such as Subhūti? And why did the sutra end abruptly with a mantra that, odd for a mantra, consisted of a string of words with clear meaning, instead of merely sacred sounds? And why was the body of the sutra apparently copied almost exactly from a Chinese translation of the "Perfection of Wisdom in Twenty-five Thousand Lines" (the "Large Sutra") done by Kumārajīva from Sanskrit over two hundred years before Xuanzang?[78] And why was Xuanzang said to have learned the sutra in China before going to India? And why was it so "Chinese" in concise structure and concentration on a

Bodhisattva—in this case Avalokiteśvara, the celestial Bodhi-sattva—then so popular in China?

With compelling deductive logic and almost lawyerly methodology, in her paper Nattier tried to find a way to *explain* the sutra's contradictions. She built a strong case for the idea that, even if the attribution to Xuanzang was true, it was actually an "apocryphal" work—in the sense that it had an introduction and conclusion created (by Xuanzang and his team) in China and a body based on Kumārajīva's earlier translation of the "Large Sutra" (which does appear to have come from India). Only later, she posited, was the Heart Sutra translated from Chinese into Sanskrit and then Tibetan, where the "framework" in the slightly longer version was edited to satisfy traditional Indian sutra conventions—by adding such things as the opening line "Thus have I heard" and terms clarifying the place (Vulture Peak) and the presence of the Buddha (not just Avalokiteśvara and Śāriputra). In the process, she also found herself agreeing with Japanese researcher Fukui Fumimasa, who theorized that what might originally have been thought of as a short *dhāraṇī*, or a condensed mnemonic device, became a true sutra. Finally, in an argument that required even more speculation and that, in her essay, even Nattier acknowledged might be harder for people to accept, she wrote (with still convincing logic), that Xuanzang himself might have translated the sutra (or "mnemonic text" or "incantation to be chanted") into Sanskrit while he was in India.

CONTROVERSY

As someone outside both academia and organized religion, trying to understand the Heart Sutra on a more personal level, I

Garage door Buddhas in Northern California.

have long been fascinated by the debate that Nattier's single paper on the Heart Sutra paper unleashed after its publication in 1992. The reaction to the paper is nearly as fascinating as the paper itself.

In the West, as in Japan, most mass-market books on the sutra try to explain its meaning, but today they may also note the controversy over its origin and mention Nattier's name. Among scholars in the West, Nattier's theory seems to be widely accepted. Yet however well reasoned, it still involves speculation, leaving plenty of room for dissent. Plenty of room, in other words, for scholars to tie themselves in knots as they try to figure out how the Heart Sutra might really have evolved. After all, any study of a text with such a long and complicated and cross-cultural history invariably involves navigating dangerous minefields. An extreme example, while not directly related to the Heart Sutra, is some of the ancient manuscripts recovered by Aurel Stein and others along the Central Asian Silk Road at the very end of the nineteenth century. Among the manuscripts were some cleverly "aged" forgeries in "unknown" languages, designed to fool experts and make money. At least one brilliant Anglo-German linguist and decipherer of exotic ancient texts, Dr. Augustus Hoernle, was bamboozled by these and—assuming them to be real—spent years trying to decipher them.[79] Still, new discoveries in the desert sands or caves of Dunhuang—and the use of advanced technologies such as A.I., big data pattern matching, and global communications—always have the potential to completely upend long-held and cherished beliefs.

On his website and in multiple articles in the *Oxford Centre for Buddhist Studies*, one of the most active and knowledgeable Anglophone researchers into the origins of the Heart Sutra is Jayarava (né Michael Attwood). A U.K.-based independent scholar of prodigious energy and intellect, he has made advocacy for Nattier's theory almost a personal crusade. Writing in a 2018 paper on the Chinese origins of the Heart Sutra, he states: "Jan Nattier's article stands out as one of the most brilliant individual contributions to 20th Century Buddhism Studies."[80]

Kazuaki Tanahashi, the Berkeley-based calligrapher and renowned translator of many Buddhist texts by the thirteenth-century Zen master Dōgen, adopts a similar view, with a compromise. In his 2014 book *The Heart Sutra: A Comprehensive*

Guide to the Classic of Mahayana Buddhism, he calls Nattier's thesis "startling" and "a revolutionary view on the formation of the sutra," a work that means "scholarly understanding about the history of the Heart Sutra will never be the same." At the time of this writing, his 268-page book was one of the few serious and detailed English-language examinations in recent years of all aspects of the sutra, not merely an "explanation" of its religious and philosophical meaning. He included different translations, including those of works that may have influenced the Heart Sutra or been incorporated into it, whether Sanskrit or Chinese or a variety of other languages. Discussion of Nattier's theory occupies over two chapters of his text, and her name is mentioned over sixty times.

Tanahashi agrees that the short version of the sutra could technically be called "apocryphal" in the traditional Chinese sense because it may not have been of Indian origin (the usual meaning of "authentic") but conceived or assembled in China. However, in considering Nattier's theory that Xuanzang may have "back-translated" the sutra into Sanskrit while in India, he takes the stance of a devotee and Zen practitioner and notes that Xuanzang could well have "received" the Sanskrit version of the sutra from Avalokiteśvara in India, as part of a mystical experience while meditating there, saying, in a sense, that the Sanskrit version could have been the product of a type of revelation. And in the midst of a very detailed analysis of Nattier's theory, he also points out an important fact: that in China at the time the role of the "translator" was not necessarily what we think it is today, that the translator was often performing a sacred act, trying to "revere and authenticate the work of their predecessors in order to secure the continuous heritage of passing down sacred texts," and making only minimal changes.[81]

In the world of recent general-audience English-language books on the sutra, Red Pine's 2004 book *The Heart Sutra: The Womb of Buddhas* has become a stand-out. It references Chinese and Sanskrit texts and includes the author's own reasoned commentaries as well as an introduction and his own new, graceful English translation of the sutra. Like Tanahashi, Red Pine comes from the world of faith and decades of Zen studies and meditation. In the introduction of his book he, too, spends several pages on Nattier's thesis. While acknowledging the "brilliance and depth of scholarship" of her work, he explains his objections, noting that we are "shown no proof that the Heart Sutra was originally composed or compiled in Chinese, that any part of the first half was extracted from the *Large Sutra* or any other Chinese text, or that the mantra was added later." In summary, he says,

> I have lingered at length over this matter because the contention that the Heart Sutra was originally compiled in China, albeit of Sanskrit pieces originally brought from India, has found a number of advocates among prominent buddhologists. Hopefully, as ancient manuscripts continue to be unearthed (alas, by explosives and those seeking sanctuary) in the region where this sutra was most likely composed, we may well see evidence someday that will clarify this issue of origin. Until then, we will have to make do with the knowledge that whoever composed this sutra bestowed on us all a great blessing.[82]

Until recently, the reaction in mainland China to Nattier's paper has been muted. Whether this is from language issues or disinterest or informational constraints in the Chinese system is not entirely clear to me, but in the Chinese diaspora the sutra has received considerable attention, accelerating in recent years. In 2012, a sixty-eight-page analysis of Nattier's work by Professor Ji Yun was published in the *Fuyan Buddhist Studies* journal in Hsinchu City, Taiwan, and subsequently translated into English by Dr. Chin Shih-Foong (with an important introduction) and published in 2017 in the Singapore *Journal of Buddhist Studies.* Author Ji, in his paper, notes that at least one Hong Kong–based scholar, Shen Jiu Cheng, had grappled with some of the same issues as Nattier as early as 1988. Ji was both critical and accepting at the same time of Nattier's thesis and in his conclusion mainly argued that more proof was needed. And as the paper's translator, Shih-Foong, noted in his introduction, Ji made a good point by saying that if the Heart Sutra were not really a true "sutra" but originally a mnemonic device called a *dhāraṇī*, then the whole issue of whether it is an "apocryphal" sutra or not could be considered largely moot.[83]

Three months after Ji Yun's paper appeared in English translation, his occasional inconsistencies and dissent from Nattier's thesis were roundly criticized by the aforementioned U.K.-based Jayarava. In his blog, Jayarava wrote a point-by-point rebuttal of over ten thousand words, over three times as long as Ji Yun's original essay. At the end of his post he noted that he had later received an email response from Ji Yun, who was horrified that he might, either because of translation or misinterpretation, have been interpreted as patronizing of Nattier, of whom he was actually a great fan.[84]

In Hong Kong, on July 22, 2019, a lecture in Cantonese on Nattier's thesis was delivered at the Centre of Buddhist Studies in Hong Kong University by Professor Henry Shiu, a Buddhist scholar from the Toronto School of Theology in Canada. With a title that translates as "The Heart Sutra, True or False," the talk description noted that in the nearly quarter century since Nattier's paper appeared it has never been firmly rebutted and appears to be gaining more and more support. On the web and in flyers, the university advertised the lecture with unintentional irony by using an image of the Heart Sutra written on something resembling palm leaves in Sanskrit from Japan's Hōryū-ji temple.[85] Long thought to be one of the oldest surviving Sanskrit copies of the sutra in the world, perhaps from India even before Xuanzang's time, in Japan it is a designated "important cultural treasure." Today, however, it is generally regarded with suspicion by scholars around the world and believed to be far more recent than originally thought, perhaps created in China a century or more after Xuanzang, and not even on real palm leaves.[86] If nothing else, the use of this image at the Hong Kong event was yet another symbol of the complexity of the Heart Sutra story. In an email to me, Professor Shiu noted that Nattier's paper is very well argued, and he stressed that in his talk he tried to focus more on how the sutra might actually have been "compiled." He told me that "99%" of the Buddhists in Hong Kong seem to never have heard of Nattier's paper," but that his talk was nonetheless attended by over two hundred people—despite the fact that Hong Kong was then in turmoil with massive daily anti-government demonstrations.[87]

REACTION IN JAPAN

In Japan, one of the first persons to comment on Nattier's paper was Fukui Fumimasa-Bunga (1934–2017), a towering figure in the study of the Heart Sutra. A man with deep knowledge of Japanese, classical Chinese, and Sanskrit (among other languages), with decades of experience in the sutra's origins and evolution, he is the author of over three huge books on it. He served for years as a professor in the Department of Eastern Philosophy at Waseda University, one of Japan's top universities, and lectured widely. He also studied for years in France and was decorated by the French government in 1991 with the *Ordre des Palmes académiques* for his academic research on Eastern religions. On top of that he was an ordained priest and holder of the *gondaisōjō*, the second-highest rank in the monastic hierarchy of Japan's Tendai (Tiantai in China) school of Mahayana Buddhism, which uses the Heart Sutra in regular practice. Most of his books include a strikingly long resume, as well as some sections written in French or Chinese or English. This undoubtedly helps deliver his opinions more widely, but in the Japanese context, at least, also betrays a slightly higher level of academic immodesty than one might expect.

Fukui's first book on the Heart Sutra was based on his doctoral dissertation of 1984, before Nattier's essay appeared. Titled *Hannya shingyō no rekishiteki kenkyū* (A historical study of the Heart Sutra), it was published in 1987, and like Nattier's essay it contained rather provocative, even disruptive, ideas for the time. Whereas most Japanese books about the Heart Sutra until then had concentrated on doctrinal aspects and interpretations, Fukui's goal was to shed light on its evolution. He used groundbreaking research and included meticulous comparisons of sutra texts from different eras and languages and versions, especially Chinese and Sanskrit. In Japan, in particular, most research on the sutra up to that point had assumed that the Heart Sutra was mainly a condensation of ideas in the huge body of Perfection of Wisdom literature (the Prajñāpāramitā sutras), and that it had become so important mainly because of its elucidation of the Mahayana concept of "emptiness" or "voidness." Most writers had also long assumed that the Chinese characters 心經 ("heart" sutra) referred to its being the "essence" of the Prajñāpāramitā sutras.

Based on years of research, and using the Dunhuang archives held in both Paris and London (where a vast number of the manuscripts taken by both Pelliot and Stein from Cave 17 in the Mogao grottos wound up), Fukui concluded that the Heart Sutra had originally been used in China mainly for its quasi-magical and incantational properties—especially those properties in the mantra—of warding off evil, eliminating fear, relieving suffering, and other tasks. And that it was only much later, during the Yuan (1271–1368) and Ming (1368—1644) dynasties, that the religious emphasis in China on the sutra shifted to stress the doctrine of "emptiness" and "voidness." Moreover, Fukui discovered, for over a century Xuanzang's translation had originally been known in China not as the "Heart Sutra" or 心経 (as it is today in China and Japan) but as 多心経, which to modern readers might be loosely interpreted as "multi-mind/heart sutra" or "multi-essence sutra" but which at the time really had a meaning closer to a *dhāraṇī*. In other words, it may not have originally been thought of as a "sutra" at all but as more of an "incantation" or "spell."[88]

Fukui's writings were an important influence on Nattier's

1992 paper, and she quoted him multiple times, so it is not surprising that he was one of the first people in Japan to read and critique it, in a 1994 lecture addressing "Current Issues in the History of Heart Sutra Research," published the same year in *Bukkyōgaku* (Journal of Buddhist Studies). For several years after that, however, Nattier's paper attracted little attention.[89]

In 2000, Fukui finally published his magnum opus, the six-hundred-plus-page *Hannya shingyō no sōgōteki kenkyū: rekishi, shakai, shiryō* (A comprehensive study of the Heart Sutra: History, society, and materials), in which he reproduced an updated version of his original 1994 paper. Approximately twenty-two pages are devoted to introducing Nattier's thesis and its context and to discussing problems in it. He notes that her thesis—that Xuanzang's Heart Sutra was an apocryphal text, probably "back-translated" by him into Sanskrit—"shocked" the academic world in Japan. But before diving into his criticisms, Fukui also lauded the work she put into her paper, agreed with much of what she said, and elsewhere was careful to recommend that others read her work and form their own conclusions, lest he might be misinterpreting some of them. His overriding issue with her work, he writes, is that

> Her logic derives from a specific set of documents, so if readers do not have enough knowledge of the history of Chinese Buddhism, and are not aware of other documents, as long as they follow along with her logic, there is a considerable danger that they will be convinced by it. Everything may make sense, but in reality, in many places ... if looking at different documents, one might come to a different opinion.[90]

Implicit throughout his critique is that her thinking has too much *rikutsu*, a convenient Japanese term meaning that she is overly prioritizing her own "logic" and "arguments." To drive the point home he lists twelve objections to her thesis, from (A) to (L). By way of example, (A) faults her for overlooking evidence that goes against her thesis; specifically, for overlooking the fact that there is no evidence in China that Xuanzang's Heart Sutra was ever regarded as "apocryphal" and that there is a vast amount of evidence to the contrary, indicating that he was indeed the translator.

In this context Fukui notes the survival of a famous inscription on a stone stele, or inscribed slab, from Xi'an that he loosely refers to as the 大唐三蔵聖教序 ("Preface to the sacred teachings [translated by] the Tripiṭaka of the Great Tang"). At the time Fukui was probably not aware of the Yunchun stele mentioned in chapter 4, carved in 661. He is here referring to a far more famous stele with a copy of the Heart Sutra inscribed on it and said to have been created in 672. A large slab 350 x 113 cm in size with a large diagonal crack, it can still be seen today in the Beilin Stele Forest museum in Xi'an.

In 648, three years after Xuanzang returned from India, Tang emperor Taizong is said to have ordered a stele created with an inscription on it commemorating Xuanzang and his contributions to Buddhism and Chinese culture. His son Gaozong (628–83), before assuming the throne the next year on his father's death, ordered another stele created with an inscription lauding both his father's work and that of Xuanzang. The stele Fukui refers to is separate and combines the father's and son's inscriptions plus Xuanzang's version of the Heart Sutra all on one stone tablet. The listed carving date,

Portion of Heart Sutra in rubbing of *Da Tang Sanzang sheng jiao xu bei* in Xi'an's Beilin Stele Forest museum. Courtesy of Special Collections, Fine Arts Library, Harvard University.

given as 672, may make it seem more recent than the Yunchun stele, but work on it actually began far earlier because of an unusual Chinese tradition. A monk named Huairen, using an extraordinarily difficult process dating back to ancient China, selected individual characters from the writing of one of the most famous calligraphers in all Chinese history—the then long-deceased Wang Xizhi (306–61)—and copied and arranged them and had them chiseled into the stele. Finding all the necessary characters (or when that was not possible assembling them from elements or radicals used in other of Wang Xizhi's characters) was an extraordinarily arduous task, said to have taken nearly twenty-five years, meaning that the actual work began while Xuanzang was still alive. The final product shows the entire Heart Sutra in only three and a half long lines, without punctuation, but it clearly lists Xuanzang as the "translator," having worked under the emperor's direction.[91]

For Fukui, the existence of a contemporary inscription, and the existence of so many ancient references in China listing Xuanzang as the sutra's "translator," was proof of its authenticity. That Nattier was not convinced by this was simply too much. In his list of objections in his book, in (K), as he wrote (using an English word), it was "unfair."[92]

To a layperson, scholars seem to have an infinite capacity for this type of argument, but to me, Fukui's strong reactions to Nattier's text go slightly beyond mere scholarly reservations. His criticism of Nattier's work concluded with an exhortation to younger Japanese Buddhologists, encouraging them to do what ought to have been obvious, namely, to study more "Sinology," especially classical Chinese language and culture and, as Japanese, to utilize their inherent strengths in Chinese characters. In what seems a bit of a nationalistic critique, he indirectly criticized North Americans and Europeans for putting too much emphasis on the study of Central Asian languages and criticized scholars who rush to study Sanskrit and Tibetan because, he says, there are far more important and accurate documents in Chinese. In between the lines, it is hard not to sense that Fukui, as a renowned scholar of a conservative older generation, in a field where most researchers have been overwhelmingly male, may not have been entirely comfortable with a paper in his field by not only a foreigner, but a scholar of another gender.

Lastly, perhaps because Fukui's main language is not English, he seems to occasionally confuse and conflate Nattier's use of the concepts "apocryphal" and "back-translation" with forgery. In her original essay, these are two separate arguments that Nattier makes about the Xuanzang Heart Sutra—(1) that it may have originated in China and (2) while acknowledging that she is going out on a limb a bit, speculating that it may even have been back-translated into Sanskrit in India by Xuanzang himself. Nattier only uses the word "forger" once in her seventy-two-page document, somewhat lightheartedly, in the sentence "If the image of Hsüan-tsang as a forger of an Indian Buddhist text seems amusing (or perhaps, to other readers, alarming), it is because it is so contrary to what the standard histories of Buddhism would lead us to expect."[93] Yet this concept of "forgery," which is very different from "apocryphal," was seized on in Fukui's writing and in Japan in general. No coincidence perhaps, but Fukui's section on Nattier in his book is titled (in his own translation) as "Jan Nattier's New Thesis: The Forged Heart Sutra in China."[94]

Criticism of Nattier soon appeared in other academic papers in Japan, usually by researchers with a religious affiliation (many Japanese private universities are run by religious groups). At the end of 2002, a paper on Japanese translations of the Sanskrit version of the Heart Sutra was published in the journal *Mikkyō bunka* (Esoteric Buddhist culture). It was written by Harada Wasō who, like Fukui, was affiliated with an esoteric Buddhist sect, in this case the Shingon school, which stresses mantras, mandalas, hand signs called *mudras*, and other esoteric elements of the faith. In his paper, Harada follows Fukui's lead and refers to Nattier's *shōgekiteki* ("shocking") back-translation theory. Like Fukui, he accuses her of cherry-picking facts to suit her theory and, in a somewhat harsh tone, directly questions her fundamental understanding of the Prajñāpāramitā sutras, stating (translated into English), "I cannot trust her ability to read Chinese documents."[95]

Jan Nattier's paper was not officially translated into Japanese until 2006, when it appeared in the *Annual of The Sanko Research Institute for the Studies of Buddhism*. Given the arcane nature of the subject matter, the use of highly technical terminology, and the different ancient languages referenced, it must have been an extraordinarily difficult task. The translators were two noted Japanese Buddhologists and experts in Sanskrit: Kudō Noriyuki, a professor at the Buddhist Sōka University, and Fukita Takamichi, an abbot in a Jōdo sect temple. They had permission to do the translation from Jan Nattier herself and had a friend of mine, Yūhō (né Thomas Kirchner), check their work. An ordained Rinzai Zen monk who has lived in Japan over fifty years and recited the Heart Sutra thousands of times as part of his daily practice, he was a meticulous proofreader. Sectarian differences in Japanese Buddhism (which is rife with differences) may be partly to blame, but oddly, in "translators' comments" by Kudō and Fukita, they state that they were not aware of any criticisms of Nattier's paper having been published in Japan since Fukui's 1994 essay—thereby implying that they were not aware of the sharply critical essay written by Fukui in his mammoth book on the sutra in 2000, as well as Harada's blisteringly critical essay of 2002.[96]

After Nattier's work was translated, she was increasingly cited in Japanese publications. In 2009, Watanabe Shōgo wrote a 376-page book about the Heart Sutra titled *Hannya shingyō: tekusuto, shisō, bunka* (The Heart Sutra: Texts, philosophy, and culture), in which he alludes to the controversy over Nattier's work without mentioning her name. The second son of the abbot of a Sōtō Zen temple in Japan, who grew up chanting the Heart Sutra, at the time of this writing Watanabe was a professor at Toyo University in Tokyo specializing in Indian Buddhism, the Prajñāpāramitā sutras, and specifically the Heart Sutra. His 2009 book was unusually accessible, even for lay people, and in it he did Japanese readers a great service by explaining the term "apocrypha." He emphasized that the word needed to be understood in a religious context, not just as "forgery" but as a description of works that, for whatever reason, do not necessarily fit into the official "canon." And these works may still be an object of worship and highly important to study. Unlike some American researchers, he adds, he does not think of the Heart Sutra as "apocryphal" but as a "solid source text" and a "representative Mahayana sutra."[97]

Most surprisingly, when I interviewed Watanabe in 2019

and asked him in more detail about Nattier's paper, he said that, while not agreeing with all of her conclusions, he has in the past used remarkably similar methodologies in comparing sutra texts (and considers Nattier a friend). In fact, in 1991, a full year before Nattier's paper appeared in English, he had published a similar paper of his own in Japan that compared the version of the Heart Sutra attributed to the famous translator Kumārajīva with Kumārajīva's translation of the voluminous *Mahāprajñāpāramitā* sutra. And Watanabe had come to the striking conclusion, as noted before, that the former was indeed an apocryphal text.[98] Today this is generally accepted theory in Japan. But Watanabe's overturning of what had been long-accepted fact in the Japanese Buddhist world never created as much controversy as Nattier's paper did.

A year after Watanabe's 2009 book, Nattier's fierce critic Harada Wasō brought out a massive 446-page tome titled *Hannya shingyō seiritsushiron: Daijō bukkyō to mikkyō no kōsaro* (Theories on the development of the Heart Sutra: At the crossroads of Mahayana and Esoteric Buddhism). It compared the Xuanzang Heart Sutra with other versions and related texts in both Chinese and Sanskrit on a word-by-word, sentence-by-sentence basis. As a scholarly study, outside of academia Harada's book on the Heart Sutra is only readable, one suspects, by obsessive Heart Sutra *otaku*/nerds with an enormous tolerance for arcane details and minutiae. He concentrates on how the key elements in the sutra, the explanatory sections and the mantra sections, developed. He sees the "sutra" as really a "patchwork" of important Mahayana influences attached to a mantra. He only occasionally mentions his disagreements with Nattier but his criticisms are considerably softened compared to his 2002 paper; indeed, in his conclusion he thanks her and states (translated) that "the existence of Dr. Nattier's sensational paper was an essential factor in the birth of this book."[99]

At the end of 2015, yet another influential paper appeared in Japan, by Ishii Kōsei, a prominent Buddhologist at Komazawa University, which is affiliated with the powerful Sōtō Zen sect. Titled *Hannya shingyō wo meguru shomondai—Jan Nattier no genjō sōsaku-setsu wo utagau* (Issues related to the Heart Sutra: Doubts about Jan Nattier's theory of its creation by Xuanzang), it took issue mainly with Nattier's theory of the Sanskrit sutra being a back-translation from Chinese. More interesting to me than the details of Ishii's argument, however, was the opening paragraph, which exemplifies what may be the prevailing attitude among Japanese Buddhologists and reveals not only their deference to senior scholars but their fears of being ignored outside of Japan. After doling out limited praise for Nattier's work and its importance, Ishii writes (in translation):

> However, it contains many points that were already known in Japan and—as both Fukui Fumimasa and Harada Wasō have already noted in great detail—her argument that Xuanzang created the Sanskrit Heart Sutra goes too far and is indeed mistaken. There is no shortage of other researchers, including in the West, who have been critical of her theory. However, it appears that since there are no papers written in English directly refuting it, when it comes to the Heart Sutra most Western Buddhologists who are not specialists in this area, as well as ordinary readers

who are interested in Buddhism, are citing her paper and regarding it as an already settled theory.[100]

Acting on these concerns, in 2016 Ishii reached out to Dr. Jeffrey Kotyk, a talented Buddhologist from Leiden (and former monk) who had been his M.A. program student at Komazawa University. When Kotyk's English translation was released on the web a year later, the non-Japanese-speaking world finally had its first real introduction to at least some Japanese criticisms, albeit in an abbreviated format.

As it turns out, in 2019 Kotyk would himself author a paper comparing Buddhist and secular accounts in China about, among other things, the relationship between Xuanzang and Emperor Taizong, as well as with Emperor Gaozong and his wife, Wu Zetian. Stripping myth and hagiography from popular accounts, he notes that toward the end of his life Gaozong was extemely ill and that most power had really passed to his powerful pro-Buddhist wife, who may have been Xuanzang's true ally, if not patron. And on the idea of whether the Heart Sutra originated in India or China, his conclusions largely align with those of Jan Nattier.[101]

A LIFE OF ITS OWN

It seems extraordinary to me that Nattier's paper, written over a quarter of a century ago—when the World Wide Web was not yet truly usable and when intertextual and interlingual research on such a niche subject was so difficult—could still be the focus of so much debate. In 1995 she wrote an eloquent and vigorous rebuttal to Fukui's twelve criticisms of her paper from the year before, ending it with a provocative statement.

Readily conceding the need for more research and hinting at some of the gender dynamics possibly involved, she wrote: "If another scholar finds a better way to account for the totality of this evidence, I will be the first to applaud her success."[102]

For reasons ultimately known only to Nattier, she never published her rebuttal, perhaps fearing it would again be misunderstood, especially in translation. Nor has she has ever written anything further on the Heart Sutra since 1992. After nearly a year of trying to meet her, in October of 2019 I finally succeeded and posed what to me has always been a burning question: Why?

> The reason is pretty simple actually: I had never planned to be a Heart Sutra specialist; this whole thing was just the result of a completely unexpected, accidental discovery. So I wrote it up and went back to the things I was normally working on (which of course have evolved over time, but not in the direction of the Heart Sutra). So it always feels a bit strange when people think I'm a "specialist" on this text![103]

In May 2019, a multi-day Buddhist studies symposium was held in Tokyo and Kyoto. The first day was titled in English, "Dismantling the *Prajñāpāramitāhṛdaya*: The Frontier of *Prajñāpāramitāhṛdaya* Studies," with lectures by noted Heart Sutra scholars in Japan (including Ishii Kosei, Watanabe Shōgo, and Saito Akira) as well as Jonathan Silk from abroad. One of the original ideas, according to Professor Watanabe (who was one of the organizers), was to have the symposium centered on

Nattier's paper and invite her. This did not materialize, but she probably would not have attended anyway because her focus by then lay elsewhere. As she said to me later that year, "At this point in my life I am totally engrossed in working on 2nd and (especially) 3rd century Chinese Buddhist translations, so I doubt very much that I will ever do anything else on the Heart Sutra again."[104]

As for Watanabe, I have always felt that in his 2009 book he provided a common-sense way for the conflicting interpretations of scholars and the faithful to coexist. He notes that Buddhism is not like Islam, which regards only the Koran as true, and that with Buddhism even teachings that evolve in a particular region outside of India may become sacred sutras in that region. As he says (in translation),

> Of course, Mahayana sutras are not sutras that Buddha himself directly taught, but having said that does not mean that all Mahayana sutras should be viewed as apocrypha. If what they say fits with early Buddhist traditions, and if, through fostering understanding and practice, they point us toward a Buddhist liberation, then we ought to view them as proper sutras.... Sutras are like "living things" that can change according to the faith of the people who believe in them.[105]

7

Heart Sutra Land

In 2018 I finally found my way to a tiny temple in the northeast corner of Nara, Japan. Officially named Kairyūō-ji, it is better known as Sumidera, "the temple in the corner." It is off the normal tourist track in a city that from 710 to 784 was the ancient capital of Japan. Other giant temples and shrines in Nara proper are often awe-inspiring World Heritage Sites, jam-packed with tourists from around the world (as well as sacred deer that famously wander freely on their grounds), but Sumidera is not like that. It is a quiet, unassuming little place with a few small ancient Buddhist buildings, including one dating back to the Nara period (710–94), set back from the paved road at the end of a long tree-lined gravel path and evocatively surrounded by old *tsuijibei*, or roofed mud walls. In recent years, Sumidera has nonetheless had a major increase in tourists, not just from Japan but also—at least prior to the 2020 pandemic—from China. They come mainly because this is where Xuanzang's Heart Sutra was first copied in quantity and diffused throughout Japan, becoming known as the "Sumidera Heart Sutra."

Buddhism was introduced into Japan via Korea around

Gateway to Sumidera.

532, but later influences came mostly from China. In Japan it had to compete with the native, animistic religion Shinto, but during the Nara period Buddhism became the state-sponsored religion, and it subsequently evolved into a dizzying number of schools and sects. Over the centuries, the authorities have at different times favored either Shinto or Buddhism and alternately treated each as either a "state religion" or deserving of suppression, yet today they are overwhelmingly the main "religions" of Japan. And the generally syncretic nature of both of them is a hallmark of modern Japanese society. The CIA World Factbook alluded to this when, in 2015, it showed 70.4% of Japanese as Shinto believers and statistically the same percentage (69.8%) as Buddhists.[106] Many of my friends have both small Shinto and Buddhist altars in their homes. And sometimes both Shinto shrines and Buddhist temples coexist on the same grounds. In part, this is because for over a thousand years the two religions often organically fused in a process called *shinbutsu shūgō*, so much so that the *Kodansha Encyclopedia of Japan* notes that "treating Shinto separately from Buddhism in the medieval period leads to gross misinterpretations of Japanese religiosity."[107]

Many of my Japanese friends will assert that Japanese in general are not very religious, yet this is only in comparison with other monotheistic cultures. In reality, Japan teems with old religions and new religions and cults and deities and spirits. Despite Christianity's high visibility in popular culture, it was banned on penalty of death for over two hundred years, and today believers amount to little more than 1% of the population. As an old missionary joke goes, Japanese get married in Shinto shrines, are buried in Buddhist ceremonies, and go to Christian churches to practice their English.

What does this all mean? One result is that Buddhist temples and texts in Japan have never undergone the massive scale of destruction that has occurred in more turbulent China, or even Korea. And the most authoritative collection of the Chinese Mahayana Buddhist canon today—the one most used by scholars around the world—is not in China or Korea but in Japan. Known in English as the *Taishō Tripiṭaka*, it was compiled between 1924 and 1934 from woodblocks stored in Korea's Haeinsa temple since 1398, from texts in China, and especially from texts that survived in Japan. It contains nearly 3,000 texts, in 85 volumes. The Xuanzang version of the Heart Sutra is found in Volume T08, Text No. 251.

Nearly all the Buddhist sects in modern Japan use the Heart Sutra —with the prominent exception of Jōdo Shinshū, one of the Pure Land sects. So, too, do many quasi-Buddhist new religions and cults. And throughout history the Heart Sutra has often been used in a Shinto context in Shinto ceremonies. To be more specific, in many ways Japan is indeed Heart Sutra land, for the Heart Sutra is so everpresent that it has almost become a religion of its own. As Jan Nattier wrote in gross understatement in the first paragraph of her provocative thesis, emphasizing the sutra's popularity throughout East Asia,

> ... the tenacity of the mass appeal of this sutra is attested by the fact that in contemporary Japan the Heart Sutra has been printed on more teacups, hand towels and neckties than has any other Buddhist scripture.[108]

When I arrived at Sumidera, I half expected to find an

ancient copy of the Heart Sutra on display, but that was not to be. Surviving copies created at the temple are important cultural assets usually stored for safekeeping elsewhere, as in the Kyoto National Museum, and only displayed occasionally at the temple. After viewing the ancient buildings on the site, I went up to the little structure near the entrance gate. As I normally do when visiting temples or shrines that I find interesting, I pulled out my temple stamp book, made of long-lasting Japanese *washi* paper, and asked the monk in the entrance structure to sign it with his calligraphy and affix the temple's stamp. Only later did I realize that he was the abbot, Ishikawa Jūgen, born into the temple and sometimes referred to in the media as an *ike jūshoku* (slang for a "hip abbot"). His "hipness" stems partly from his efforts in reaching out to new, younger audiences with modern media and for his friendship with at least one famous manga artist, Miura Jun, who has also authored a photo-art book on the Heart Sutra.

Buddhism in Japan has often been associated with the end-stage of life. Thanks to Japan's rapidly aging population, when compared with Buddhism in other countries (in Southeast Asia or even North America, for example) it has increasingly been described by scholars as "funerary Buddhism." Related to this is a parallel tendency among young people to think of Buddhism in general as "stuffy," "dreary," or even a bit "morbid," so progressive priests have to work hard to attract young people. At Sumidera, Ishikawa was early to use a website and social and other modern media technology to reach out to a younger audience.

Two pamphlets Ishikawa gave me about his temple revealed his modern approach. They were in manga format—brightly colored, eight-page comic books—and both had a slangy title (in translation) of "Awesome Facts About ...," one focusing on the temple and the other on its most famous eighth-century abbot, Genbō. Since Japan is the world's capital of manga, this made sense, since manga are not just entertainment but one of the main sources of information for modern citizens. In one of the comic books, the current abbot, Ishikawa, is shown praying in the temple, carrying on a 1,300-year-old tradition, but there are also maps showing tourists how to reach the temple, along with pleas for broader recognition of the temple's historical value.

I learned a lot, in a hurry, from the twin manga. The temple had close links with the official spread of Buddhism in Japan in the early eighth century. The emperor Shōmu, who reigned from 724 to 749, and his empress, Kōmyō, were both devout Buddhists and were instrumental in the construction of a national network of temples and nunneries, including Tōdai-ji, one of the grandest temple complexes in Nara, if not all Japan. Sumidera became an official temple of the empress Kōmyō and was used to pray for the well-being of the imperial family.

During the Nara period Tang China was the center of the Asian world, and numerous emissary-monks or *kentōshi* from the Japanese court made the arduous and treacherous journey across the sea to study and return home with Chinese Buddhism and culture. Genbō and three others left the imperial capital on a 717 mission and studied hard under Chinese masters. Genbō's talents, in particular, were recognized by the then-Tang emperor, giving him access to the center of power. In the process, he also came to realize that in China Buddhism was more than just a religion; it was also an important tool used to rule the country. In the Sumidera manga, after nearly twenty years of study Genbō is shown returning to Japan on a ship that is caught in a treacherous storm. On deck he prays for salvation by reciting the "Dragon King of the Sea" sutra. When the Japanese emperor and empress heard that this rather obscure sutra, about Buddha preaching to the Naga-Dragon King, had protected Genbō, they decided that Sumidera should be given the official name it has today, based on the Chinese characters for ocean-dragon-king-temple and their Japanese pronunciation: Kairyūō-ji. Genbō was appointed abbot and, because he was devoted to Xuanzang's version of the Heart Sutra, he initiated mass copying of it. As a result, the manga notes, nearly a hundred percent of all sutra copying subsequently done in Japan has been based on what is known as the *Sumidera shingyō*, the "Sumidera Heart Sutra."

Genbō was ultimately caught up in court intrigues and sent or exiled to the southern island of Kyushu, where he disappeared from history. But the last page of the comic about him lists his accomplishments: he brought back five thousand fascicles or volumes of sutras from China; he helped to build the giant Buddha statue in Tōdai-ji and a national network of temples; he introduced Chinese-court-style Buddhism; he helped introduce esoteric Buddhism into Japan; and, perhaps more than anything else, he promoted mass copying of the Heart Sutra at Sumidera as well as the practice of chanting it.[109]

Heart Sutra expert Professor Watanabe notes that there are written records of Xuanzang's sutra being copied in Japan as early as 731, only eighty-two years after Xuanzang's edition appeared in China, and of it being commonly recited only a few years after that. But it was the Sumidera copies that had by far the most impact because of the scale of the effort and the backing of the imperial court. Kūkai (774–835)—a monk and towering intellectual who also studied in China—is today regarded as a saint because of his founding of the Shingon school of mantra-*mudra*-mandala-centered esoteric Buddhism. He, too, studied briefly at Sumidera, and while there he reportedly made one hundred copies of the sutra each day, for a total of over a thousand. Later, his commentary—*Hannya shingyō hiken,* or "Secret Key to the Heart Sutra"—would become arguably the most famous commentary on the Heart Sutra in all of Japan.[110]

The Heart Sutra first spread rapidly in Japan through state sponsorship. Successive emperors and nobles in the Nara period actively embraced it, encouraging organized copying and—as with Emperor Junnin on August 18, 758—sometimes issuing edicts that all subjects should chant it whenever they could. Often, in the Nara and later eras, it was hoped this would help ward off pestilence and famine and promote general prosperity. Belief in the merits of the sutra subsequently spread through the aristocracy and into the samurai class, with sutras being copied and richly decorated. And as its use broadened, the sutra was also regularly recited or even copied at large religious gatherings in temples (and sometimes even shrines) throughout the year. This was generally done in accordance with the calendar, to ward off misfortune and accrue merit. As belief in the efficacy of the sutra percolated into the general populace, copying and reciting it came to be used in deathbed ceremonies, memorial services, ancestor worship, exorcism, and as a *dhāraṇī* or spell to pacify vengeful spirits.[111]

Today, chanting is widely done in temples in Japan by

monks. Daigaku Rummé, who spent twenty-seven years in eastern Japan in a remote Sōtō Zen temple named Hosshin-ji, recalls the routine there as follows, noting that it was one of the most frequently chanted of all sutras:

> [The Heart Sutra] is chanted as part of the morning service which is done after one period of zazen, and before breakfast. It is specifically part of the *Ogu Fugin*, which is the sutra dedicated to all Arhats (those worthy of receiving offerings).... The Heart Sutra is chanted at various other times, too. For example, the dedication to *Idatenson*, guardian of the kitchen, and at many other ceremonies, both big and small. And when we went on *aki takuhatsu* [begging for alms in the autumn], we would chant sutras in front of homes and businesses, at which time we could chant whichever sutra we chose, and I often chanted the Heart Sutra then, too.[112]

Of course, the Heart Sutra is not just chanted by monks, but also by ordinary people as a way to gain merit, improve their karma, and improve their lives. Most pilgrims on the famous eighty-eight temple pilgrimage in Shikoku Island chant it at every stop. Even at ordinary temples visitors may be encouraged to join in, creating a vibrational harmony. But there is of course lots of chanting also done by people at home in front of a small altar (or anywhere, for that matter). For those who don't want to rely on a printed version, the sutra is short enough to memorize (although doing so, I can attest, takes a certain intellectual effort and discipline and time).

As noted previously, save for a few minor orthographic changes the Japanese written sutra is identical to the original Xuanzang version in China. One might think that it would therefore be vastly easier for Chinese mainlanders to read the sutra, but this is not necessarily true. The Chinese language in the year 649 was a very different animal from the Chinese of today in both grammar and pronunciation. And in one small way it may be even be a bit harder for mainlanders to read now. Since the 1949 revolution, mainland schools have taught a drastically simplified character set—one that looks very different from the traditional one that comprises the Chinese characters used in 649. The character string 遠離 ("far away," or "removed from"), for example, is now written as 远离. True, it may now possible to push a button on a computer and convert traditional characters to the new simplified versions, or even fairly easy to teach oneself how to read older characters. But to natives of Japan and Taiwan and Hong Kong—where children learn a much more traditional character set—most of the characters in the sutra look almost exactly as they did 1,400 years ago.

On the other hand, when the Heart Sutra is recited today in Japan, the Chinese characters or ideograms are given Japanese, not Chinese, pronunciations. And this creates a different obstacle for chanters. Japanese is an utterly different language from Chinese, not even sharing the same linguistic roots; it only shares the characters, and to do that it must use some clever tricks devised centuries ago. Even the title of the Heart Sutra—the *Prajñāpāramitā Hṛdaya*—sounds radically different in modern Mandarin Chinese and in Japanese. In Chinese it is *Bōrěbōluómìduō xīngjíng*. In Japanese it is *Hannya haramita shingyō*. This means that reciting the sutra in Japanese requires a compromise. In China, each ideogram usually has only one syllable, but for some Chinese characters Japanese uses two syllables, which changes the rhythm. An example is the famous phrase 色不異空, or "Form is not different from emptiness." In modern Mandarin this is pronounced *Sè-bú-yì-kōng*, but in Japanese it is *shiki-fu-i-kū*, the first character—色 or "form"—being pronounced *shiki*, requiring two syllables.

Differences in pronunciation aside, in Japan the sound of the words themselves is often regarded as sacred, which gives vocalization an added power. In a sense, this resembles what in Shinto is called *kotodama* (言霊), written with the characters for "speech" and "spirit," reflecting the belief that words have power or a spirit of their own and that vocalizing them can influence and alter physical reality. This is particularly true with the esoteric schools of Buddhism in Japan, where words possess an almost magical quality and where one hears mentions of "seeing the sound"—one can even find people disciplining themselves in winter chanting the Heart Sutra and praying under freezing cold waterfalls, among other spiritual exercises. Something similar is emphasized at even less-esoteric schools. As Yamada Hōin, a long-term priest at Nara's Yakushi-ji temple of the Hossō sect, recounted in a 2010 interview (translated),

> The Heart Sutra is the culmination of Lord Buddha's wisdom, so there is profound meaning in each of the words in the sutra. Of course, there is power in the text itself, but independent of that there is power in the sound…. [Of the mantra, for example], even if we

don't understand its meaning at all, we can feel its
beauty in the sound alone. It's almost as though the
gratitude for Xuanzang, who transcribed the sounds
so long, long ago, is transmitted down to us here
today.[113]

For those attempting to chant the sutra who don't know
how to read or pronounce all the characters, there is no short-
age of modern printed texts to help. One of the most novel
approaches was developed in rural Japan during the Edo
period, in the early 1700s, at a time when illiteracy was still
common, especially in remote, mountainous areas. Since the
faithful often could not read the original Chinese characters in
the Heart Sutra—or even the *hiragana* phonetic script attached
to the characters as a pronunciation key—versions were created using tiny images as a mnemonic aid. In 2012, Watanabe
Shōgo published *Etoki hannya shingyō* (Explaining The Heart
Sutra in pictures), a book in which he reproduced some of
these early examples. In the feudal era's Morioka domain, for
example, the *para* in Prajñāpāramitā was assigned an image of
a large stomach, because in Japanese a common but vulgar way
of saying stomach is *hara*, which is close to the way the Sanskrit
sound *para* was presumably vocalized. Similarly, the *sa* sound
in Bodhisattva is represented with a dog pissing, because in
local dialect the normal Japanese sound of a dog urinating, シ
ッ or *shi!*, was then pronounced サツ or *sa!*[114]

Rather than instruct illiterate farmers about "emptiness"
and transcendental wisdom, these "visual Heart Sutras" helped
them learn how to chant it, again showing indirectly how the
"sound" of the sutra was as important as the "understanding"

of it. With a boom in interest in the Heart Sutra in the last twenty years or so, one can now purchase all sorts of items with these old visual Heart Sutras reproduced. At home, among my growing collection of Heart Sutra paraphernalia, I have a lovely towel, bought at the Nara National Museum souvenir shop, as well as a box of band-aids with a visual Heart Sutra design.

Today easy-to-download smart phone apps give hints on how to memorize passages and show how to recite them. In the Chinese diaspora one can readily buy or download the sound of monks in temples chanting the Heart Sutra as part of their daily ritual. The sutra has also been widely put to music on YouTube by both monks and laity, the latter occasionally doing their own techno-rap remix versions. In Japan, one of the most successful recent musical renditions is by the Rinzai Zen sect vice-abbot mentioned in chapter 4, Yakushiji Kanhō. He plays an electric guitar, and his singing/chanting uses a simple repetitive melody with a background beat—evoking temple chanting while appealing to modern sensibilities. He recites/sings the entire sutra in only about 2.5 minutes, which is faster than most temple chanting, and by slowly adding layers of chorus he creates a beautiful, mounting tension that climaxes with the mantra. In 2018, he released an entire album called *Heart Sutra* with eleven different tracks on it, all titled "Heart Sutra," all remix versions.[115]

It is not necessary to go very far out of one's way to hear the Heart Sutra being chanted in Japan. It is frequently chanted at homes and temples and at special concerts and is a staple of background music ("BGM") in popular culture movies and television shows, used whenever the creators want a soundtrack that can quickly evoke Buddhism or Japanese religiosity.

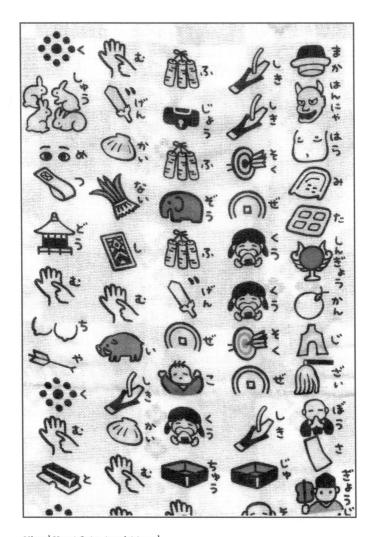

Visual Heart Sutra tourist towel.

SUTRA COPYING

Copying the sutra, in addition to chanting it, is a way to achieve karmic merit. We have already seen how ordinary people practice copying the Xuanzang version of the sutra at home, but many religious sects now offer special places to copy it on their temple grounds. For a small fee they provide ink and brushes (or pencil or ballpoint pens for the less confident) and special paper that allows unfamiliar ideograms to be carefully traced. Along with regular donations and the usual selling of amulets, trinkets, prayer books, and prayer services, sutra copying is now often a source of revenue for temples. Larger ones sometimes have entire halls dedicated to sutra copying with beautiful statues of Buddha on display to establish a meditative mood. By attaching a wish of some sort at the end of the sutra (along with the copier's name and date), the calligraphic act becomes a votive act, expressing hopes to pass exams, keep families and ancestors safe, and ensure general happiness and good health. At these *shakyō-e*, or "sutra copying gatherings," other sutras may also be copied, but because of its ubiquity and brevity the Heart Sutra is invariably the most popular.

Over the centuries, sutra copying has become a highly ritualized art form. The best copiers obviously have admirable calligraphic skills, but not everyone is a calligrapher. In 2019, one website in Japan named Shakyōya, or "The Sutra Copy Place," was selling all the utensils one might need, from ink to ink rubbing stones, brushes, and papers. It also provided a list of different ways of copying: express thanks three times after writing each character, have multiple people cooperate to copy a sutra, and so forth.

For priests and monks, the copying process can be even

more ritualized. One book I own has detailed descriptions of ideal locations for copying (temples in the mountains, away from phones and so on), the best implements to use, clothes and accessories to wear or not wear (no wristwatches), positions to assume, and ways to make corrections; it discusses the need for bowing as well as personal cleanliness and wearing face masks for the sake of purity.[116]

The ink for sutra copying is usually black and the paper white, but sometimes gold or silver ink is used to apply characters to darker, decorative color paper. I have multiple books on Heart Sutra copying, and while all demonstrate the proper calligraphic techniques, some also show how to make *konshikindei* sutras, with gold-colored ink on deep blue paper. Hasedera is a famous and beautiful Shingon sect temple in Kamakura, popular among Japanese and visitors from China and Korea. Reportedly built on the order of Nara-period Emperor Shōmu in 736, it today has its own sutra-copying hall, where in addition to regular fee-based copying it offers those more experienced everything needed for *konshikindei* copying. The space is quite a contrast to the temple's main hall, where visitors can enjoy a far more rudimentary form of sutra copying—a vastly simpler way of acquiring merit—by taking a single small flat stone from a pile and writing upon it a single character in the proper order, thus with other visitors collectively recreating the entire sutra.

In almost all these spiritual exercises, the Sumidera version of the Heart Sutra, or what is essentially the Xuanzang version, is used as a master reference. Following the Sumidera format, one usually writes from right to left, in vertical top-to-bottom columns of seventeen characters each, except for the mantra portion. Each seventeen-character column is usually separated by faint lines, which can be seen on an original Sumidera copy in the Kyoto National Museum, a vestigial reference to the fact that many ancient Buddhist sutras in China were once copied not on paper but vertically on small thin slats of wood or bamboo that were strung together with string and rolled up into a convenient bundle.

The Heart Sutra has not always been written in ink. In 2009 I visited a special exhibit at the Tokyo University of the Arts museum, titled "A Hidden Heritage—Treasures of Japanese Imperial Convents." The convents were for aristocrat women who had shaved their heads and renounced the world. The exhibit featured mainly lovely artifacts from their daily lives, but one of the most striking was a version of the Heart Sutra rendered in blood as an act of extreme devotion. Called *kessho*, it was an especially profound way of "copying" the Heart Sutra; the blood usually came from a self-inflicted cut in the thumb, in this case that of the Abbess Daitsū Bunchi in the seventeenth century, at Enshō-ji, a Rinzai Zen sect convent in Nara. Today, needless to say, this is not the normal way the Heart Sutra is written, but it remains an extreme option.

CHANNELING THROUGH CALLIGRAPHY

Just as it is not necessary to intellectually "understand" the sutra when chanting it, neither is it necessary to understand the sutra when copying it, because both are religious acts involving a type of meditation. This was made clear to me when, in 2018, I visited a beautiful Rinzai Zen sect temple named Ryōun-ji (written with the characters for dragon-cloud-temple). Ryōun-ji is in Hamamatsu, Shizuoka Prefecture, a city once famous for textiles, pianos, and motorcycle manufacturing, all now in decline because of competition from lower-wage nations. Like many temples in other areas of Japan, the friendly young priest-couple who operate the temple needed something to appeal to both existing and potentially new, hopefully young, parishioners.

Ryōun-ji offers the usual Buddhist funerary and memorial services in addition to a large ossuary for the cremated. But it also has classes in *zazen*, sutra copying, and ritualized chanting of Buddhist hymns for good health, as well as gardening on the large temple grounds, opportunities to take temple-sponsored trips, Pilates classes for women needing mind-body alignment, and—in what is a relatively new focus in Japanese Buddhist temples, which have concentrated more on end-of-life services—helping single people find mates. Yet more than anything else, the highlight of Ryōun-ji—advertised on large posters on the street in front of the temple—is what it claims is the world's largest Heart Sutra.

Whether the Ryōun-ji Heart Sutra is literally the world's largest or not is subject to debate. The Nung Chan Monastery of the Dharma Drum sect in Taipei, Taiwan, has a giant Heart Sutra wall, but its sutra characters are essentially cutouts that let natural light through the wall cast a shifting pattern on the hall's floor. The Fo Guang Shan monastery sutra repository hall in Kaohsiung, Taiwan, also has an enormous wall devoted to the sutra, but its characters, while looking as though brush painted, are etched into the wall, copied from the calligraphy of the sect's master and then magnified many times over.

The Ryōun-ji wall-sutra is completely different. It was created in 2017 by then thirty-year-old calligrapher Kanazawa

The Heart Sutra of Kanazawa Shōko at Ryōun-ji, shown by Abbot Kimiya.

Shōko, who has Down's syndrome. When I visited the temple the charismatic and young abbot, Kimiya Kōshi, led me into a large, newly constructed hall, appropriately named the "Nirvana Hall," where the sutra was on display. Of unpainted wood construction, with a floor of tatami mats, the hall emitted a clean and natural feeling that such Japanese interiors often generate. But I was most struck by the sutra's beauty. To me, the calligraphy exuded an enormous, mysterious power.

The sutra follows the standard format used by individuals at home or at temples, except that it is huge—4 meters wide by 16 meters long—and most lines are twelve boldly written characters in length. Although it has no punctuation, specific sections are subtly spaced, perhaps for easier understanding of their meaning. It would have been extremely difficult, if not impossible, to calligraphically render the sutra with brush and ink directly on the wall itself, so instead Kanazawa first executed the black characters in bold strokes with an enormous brush, held with both hands, slapping ink generously on large stretches of bright white paper stretched on the floor. These sections were then carefully glued together by highly skilled craftsmen to form a giant surface covering most of the Nirvana Hall wall. The paper is subtly bordered by an unobtrusive wood frame, which is in turn set against a black wall for dramatic highlight.

As Kimiya described it to me, Kanazawa's mother was an extremely talented calligrapher, and when she realized that her daughter had a remarkable ability she began teaching her. Kanazawa began to enjoy calligraphy. Even though she could not really understand the meaning of the characters, she learned to love the process of writing them. Her approach to calligraphy was unique. She was not doing it for money, since she had no concept of what money was. She was not doing it for fame, because she had no concept of that, either. She was doing it simply because it made her, her mother, and those around her, happy. In other words, she was writing with a truly pure and unsullied heart, almost exemplifying the Mahayana Buddhist concept of "nothingness" or "voidness" that the Heart Sutra emphasizes. In fact, one of her favorite characters is 無— in Buddhism "non-existence" or "negation," pronounced *mu* in Japanese or *wu* in Chinese.

Kanazawa's calligraphy has a remarkably consistent style, with horizontal strokes rising slightly to the right and—because she draws single strokes without stopping to redip her brush—a remarkably attenuated gradation. This, plus her ability to concentrate in a way that most ordinary people cannot, gives her calligraphy a mysterious emotive power. The purity of her approach, and the scale of her calligraphy, according to Kimiya, is sometimes overwhelming for visitors. Some try to emulate her calligraphy with notepads. Others are so deeply moved that they weep. When I viewed it, the impact was amplified by the sound of a memorial service held right in front of the wall, with people chanting the Heart Sutra.

Save for the title variation, the usual Japanese addition of two minor characters mentioned in chapter 3, and the last line, where Kanazawa has written her name and age, her sutra is the same as that produced by Xuanzang 1,400 years ago and the same as the Sumidera version. As with other Heart Sutra scrolls and walls and paraphernalia, that all also makes sense because Xuanzang, or at least part of him, is also in Japan. It was that connection that eventually led me to my first personal experience of official Heart Sutra calligraphy at a temple.

XUANZANG IN JAPAN

The Chinese name Xuanzang is pronounced *Genjō* in Japanese, and the main repository of Xuanzang relics in Japan is reputedly at the Genjō pagoda near Jion-ji temple in Iwatsuki in the northeastern corner of Saitama City. Iwatsuki is a somewhat inconvenient hour or more outside of Tokyo. Part of Xuanzang's skull is said to be enshrined there, too, but when I first heard this claim I thought it could not be entirely serious. After all, how could Xuanzang have wound up in Japan?

Was it a claim like that made by another town in far northern Japan, that it had the grave of Jesus Christ? When I finally visited Jion-ji in 2019, however, I realized that there was quite a backstory to it all.

The Jion-ji temple is thought to have been established between 824 and 834. It is affiliated with the Tendai (Tiantai, in China) sect of Buddhism, and the main focus of worship is the "thousand arm" god/dess of mercy (Avalokiteśvara). The characters of "Jion" (慈恩) are the same as those for the great Ci'en monastery in Chang'an (Xi'an)—built by the Tang emperor for Xuanzang after his return from India. The Jion-ji temple's founder had selected the name because he had studied in Chang'an, China, in his youth and felt that the Iwatsuki area in Japan resembled it.

The Genjō pagoda is on a tiny elevated area with a few trees, a short walk on a winding, narrow path from the temple across a road and through some rice fields. A relatively new, brightly colored, and rather Chinese-looking gate officially fronts the area, flanked by plum trees that blossom beautifully early in the spring. Immediately inside the gate is a bronze statue of Xuanzang with his elaborate backpack, a descriptive plaque, a map detailing his amazing journey from Tang China to India and back, some decorative flags, offering and incense boxes, flower vases, and a thirteen-stage (or "story") pagoda. Over 15 meters in height, the pagoda was not as impressive as I had imagined and pales in comparison to the 64-meter-tall current version of the Giant Wild Goose Pagoda built for Xuanzang in Xi'an by the Tang emperor. The Genjō pagoda's fame rests not on its height but on the belief that it contains part of Xuanzang's skull, a lure to devotees who come before it, as I did, to pray or recite the Heart Sutra. That it was built in 1950, shortly after World War II, when Japan was under the Occupation and in extreme poverty, may have something to do with the quasi-modern but rudimentary look of the granite structure. But how did part of Xuanzang's skull wind up inside it? When I pressed the temple monks for information, they gave me an easy-to-understand booklet, obviously created in response to endless queries by curious visitors.

The pamphlet revealed that, on December 23, 1942, during the Japanese occupation of Nanjing, members of an Imperial Army unit led by Lt. Colonel Takamori Ryūsuke were doing some construction work. To their surprise, they unearthed a small stone sarcophagus, about 16 by 160 centimeters in size, inside which they found another small stone casket. Inside that were funereal inscriptions carved during two different dynasties, in 1027 and 1386, part of a skull, and several funereal objects. Having heard that there had once been an important temple in the area, Takamori contacted the Nanjing puppet government. A bevy of scholars were able to decipher the inscriptions—which specifically mentioned that the relics are those of Xuanzang—and to determine that they were indeed looking at parietal bones from Xuanzang's skull (or at least what was described as such). Takamori immediately sent everything he had found to the Nanjing government. The government, overjoyed, started a movement to construct a "Xuanzang" pagoda in Nanjing for the objects, which, with the aid of the Imperial Army, was completed and celebrated in an elaborate ceremony on October 10, 1944. Various dignitaries, including representatives of the Japan Buddhist Federation, were in attendance, and (according to the booklet) it was here on the 23rd that a portion of the skull material was handed over and taken back to Tokyo under guard.[117]

At that point, Tokyo was being bombed daily by American B-29s, so desperate attempts were made to find a safe place for the relics. At first they were shuffled among multiple temples in the Tokyo area, but all turned out to be too near bombing targets. Eventually, they wound up in Jion-ji, in the Iwatsuki area of Saitama where they are now. When the war ended and the Japanese empire collapsed, disagreements arose about the provenance of the bone relics. This is understandable, given fears in Japan, especially, that they might be regarded as stolen war-booty (which, of course, they were). Concerned about the implications of all of this, in 1946 the Japan Buddhist Federation was able to contact Chiang Kai-shek, the then-beleaguered president of Kuomintang China, who was about to be defeated in a civil war by Mao Zedong's Red Army and flee to the island of Taiwan. According to the Jion-ji booklet, Chiang Kai-shek welcomed the enshrinement of the relics in the Jion-ji temple in Japan, in part because of the serendipitous historical connection with the Ci'en temple in China (at least in terms of the name) and because he thought it would be good for postwar Japanese-Chinese relations.[118]

Nothing is as simple as it seems, of course, and some of the awkward problems have been, if not solved, at least ameliorated by a system known as *bunkotsu* in Japan—literally, the "dividing of bones," a way of sharing ashes and relics in multiple locations. Some of Xuanzang's remains were memorialized at the time of his death at a temple in Xi'an. After 1944, when his skull was discovered by the Imperial Army in Nanjing, some portions were also given to other temples in China, in

Beijing, Tianjin, Sichuan, and Guangzhou. Many Chinese sites and relics were severely damaged or lost in the 1966–76 Cultural Revolution. In 1955, Taiwan asked Jion-ji for some relics and in 1974 so did Yakushi-ji temple in Japan's ancient capital of Nara. According to a book issued by Yakushi-ji itself, Xuanzang's relics are today scattered and memorialized in over nine places, in China, Japan, Taiwan, and even in Nalanda, India.[119]

SUTRA COPYING AT YAKUSHI-JI

After visiting Jion temple near Tokyo, I traveled to Nara again to visit Yakushi-ji temple. I had been to Yakushi-ji several times before, but I now better understood why it had requested to share in Xuanzang's relics. It is registered as a UNESCO World Heritage Site and is thought to date back to 680, when the emperor Tenmu directed it to be constructed in hopes that it might save his ailing wife. He never saw it completed, but his wife, Jitō, survived to become Japan's forty-first monarch and third actual reigning empress (as opposed to consort). Moved to its current site from Japan's first capital in nearby Kashihara in 710, the temple today is the headquarters of what is known as the Hossō sect in Japan, otherwise known as Yogācāra, imported from India and China.

Yogācāra is one of the major Mahayana schools of Buddhism and was especially promoted in China by Xuanzang on his return from India, where it had been developing since the fourth century. It encompasses a sometimes head-spinning philosophy that hints at the illusory nature of our perceived reality. As Damien Keown et al.'s *A Dictionary of Buddhism* explains it, "in Japan, the philosophy was also known in Japanese as *yuishiki*, or 'consciousness-only,' because of its fundamental belief that all of reality, including both the objective world and the subjective mind that regards it, are but evolutions of consciousness according to karma."[120]

In 653 the Japanese priest Dōshō (629–700) went to China as part of an early group of emissary-scholars, studied Yogācāra directly under Xuanzang (who is said to have taken a great liking to him), and brought back numerous sutras to Japan, where he helped popularize both Yogācāra and Zen philosophy. In 698, Dōshō was appointed the first high priest in Japan to consecrate a needlework tapestry of Amida Buddha in a newly completed hall at Yakushi-ji; in accordance with his will, on his death the following year it is reported that he had the first Buddhist cremation in Japan.[121]

With this connection, and with the relics received from the smaller Jion temple, Yakushi-ji has gone all-out on Xuanzang and the Heart Sutra. Yakushi-ji is described as a "temple," but it is really a vast complex and even includes a Shinto shrine. There are parking lots for cars and tourist buses; an entrance fee of about $16 was charged when my wife and I visited. We started out with a lecture by a monk who delivered a short sermon on the history of the temple and on the merits of copying sutras and making donations in general. The monk was well rehearsed and humorous, and he pointedly explained that, unlike most Buddhist temples, Yakushi-ji is not supported by a *danka* system, or registry of parishioner households. It exists today on donations. This frees it from the sometimes dreary and funerary-centric aspects of many temples, but makes it more reliant on tourism and, increasingly, on people paying for the privilege of sutra copying in a hall specially designed for that purpose.

Save for the east pagoda, almost all the original build-ings in Yakushi-ji have been lost in accidents, wars, or natu-ral disasters, but they have been slowly rebuilt over the years to restore the complex to its former glory. And since 1968 sutra copying has been a way to pay for it. In 1991, the new "Xuanzang precinct" area of the complex (as it is referred to in English signage for tourists) was completed, by which time over five million sutra copies had already been collected. The area includes a two-story octagonal pagoda that houses the relics from Jion-ji as well as a very realistic icon-statue of a solid-looking Xuanzang sitting cross-legged. His left hand holds a sheath of palm-leaf sutras from India, and his right hand a brush so that he can write the Chinese translation on paper in front of him. Visitors can pray and offer incense and money to his spirit.

A special hall was created in the same area in 2000 to showcase mural paintings by the famous *nihonga* artist Hirayama Ikuo. By that time seven million sutra copies had been made. Hirayama, a survivor of the atomic bombing of Hiroshima, developed a life-long interest in Buddhism and Xuanzang, and his huge, spectacular paintings show dreamlike scenes from Xuanzang's travels along the Silk Road and over the Hindukush Mountains to India. They include images of the Taklamakan desert ruins of Gaochang, towering Himalayan mountain ranges, the Giant Wild Goose Pagoda in Xi'an, and the giant Bamiyan Buddha statues in Afghanistan as they must have looked to Xuanzang—over 1,400 years before the Taliban destroyed them in 2001.

My main focus at Yakushi-ji was on the sutra copy-ing hall because I had heard that Yakushi-ji's approach had

Statue of Xuanzang translating Sanskrit sutras into Chinese at Yakushi-ji.

helped trigger a national boom in sutra copying, especially of the Heart Sutra. In his book *The Heart Sutra: A Comprehensive Guide to the Classic of Mahayana Buddhism*, Kaz Tanahashi, the Berkeley-based calligrapher and translator/author, has a wonderful account of his experience in the same hall in 2002. But Tanahashi is a gifted professional calligrapher. I approached the experience as a complete neophyte, someone who knows how to write Japanese but—after years of using a word processor—has zero brush calligraphy skills and whose handwriting in both Japanese and English is now barely legible.

There are several protocols to be followed in copying sutras at Yakushi-ji. The first is to pay money. There are four sutras offered, with templates provided to copy over on Japanese paper. The Xuanzang version of the Heart Sutra is by far the most popular and, at around $20, the best deal. After taking off your shoes in the hall entrance, putting some clove spice in your mouth, purifying yourself with incense, you put on a *wakesa*—in this case a Buddhist sash draped around the neck—and enter. The sash, it should be noted, has inscriptions in Chinese characters praying for the reconstruction of Yakushi-ji on one side and for a million copies of sutras on the other. The room is large, with a tatami grass mat floor, upon which red carpet has been laid, leaving space for tables and chairs so that one's feet can always be on tatami. Nearly two hundred people can copy sutras at once, facing a statue of Buddha flanked by two Bodhisattvas and fronted by flowers, offering boxes, and trays in which to place completed sutras. To encourage repeat copying of sutras, those who do three get a temple stamp book, those who do 108 get a neck sash, and those who do 216 are presented with a *kataginu*, or sleeveless robe.

Most people place the sutra template on the tabletop, lay the lined *washi* paper provided on top of it, and then trace the sutra characters on the paper. Because Japanese black *sumi* ink can easily last over a thousand years, brushes are provided and recommended, along with rubbing stones and ink sticks. But in what may be a concession to modern, computer/ cell-phone-addled youth, pencils are also allowed. My wife, raised Chinese and a student of calligraphy, chose the brush and ink whereas I, unhesitatingly, chose pencil.

It is possible to do the sutra in stages and even come back another time to finish, but I was in a hurry. I had often copied the sutra at home, so I raced through the exercise, finishing before my wife, whose beautiful rendition of the Heart Sutra looked far better than mine. I put my name and the date at the end, and a customary wish (for family health and happiness in this case), and placed the scroll in the appropriate bin. Everything in the process might seem ritualized, even somewhat commercialized, but I could feel, in my own tiny way, what it was all about. I had completely lost myself in the process of writing and left the hall with my mind more focused and calmer than when I started.

8

The Metaphysical Can Opener

I first met Mori Masahiro in the spring of 1986, when interviewing scientists for my book *Inside the Robot Kingdom: Japan, Mechatronics, and the Coming Robotopia.* Mori's focus was on robots and Buddhism, which seemed a novel combination to me at the time. He turned out to be one of the most memorable people I have ever met. He was already recognized for his research into models of the human finger and hands and then for walking mechanisms, robots for industry, autonomous robots, and starting robot contests. Unusual for a Japanese scientist at the time, he already had a name overseas.

In researching robots Mori had found that he had to understand not only the human body's individual parts and their functions but their relationship to the entire human body and the universe in which it exists. And this had brought him to Buddhism, which teaches that the Buddha-nature is in all things (not just sentient beings) and is where, according to his interpretation, parts of whole systems are simultaneously independent and connected—that a universe and the source of all truth can exist in the single petal of a flower. Only a few years earlier, a book of his essays had been translated and published in English with the provocative title of *The Buddha in the Robot: A Robot Engineer's Thoughts on Science and Religion.*

Mori, a ninety-two-year-old with a razor-sharp mind at the time of this writing, is a long-time student of Buddhism—especially the Rinzai sect of Zen Buddhism, which delights in shaking rigid human minds with riddles and paradoxes, thus allowing new truths to emerge and lead us to enlightenment. In a more immediate sense, Mori's main goal in using Buddhism has been to stimulate creative thinking, to get people to think "outside of the box." It is, he might say, a type of "applied Buddhism."

Always smiling, in the course of our 1986 interview he pulled out an ordinary permanent-ink magic marker and lit it with a lighter, whereupon he announced with delight, "See? It's not a marker, it's really a lamp!" It was only one of many intellectual tricks he played with ordinary objects in his office to try to get me to perceive things differently. I mentioned in passing that I had a copy of the Heart Sutra on my wall at home, but the focus of our conversation at the time was on robots. Mori is a fan of multiple Mahayana sutras (especially the Diamond and Lotus sutras), and he sometimes even complains that the Heart Sutra's obtuse brevity makes it hard to understand. But this is all said with an understated humor, for the Heart Sutra is indeed a drastic crystallization of the ideas in the vastly larger Prajñāpāramitā sutras. It is also so popular in Japan that, in conversation, at least, Mori the roboticist may perversely be reluctant to emphasize how much his thinking is actually influenced by it.

In my interview, Mori provocatively stated that "to learn the Buddhist way is to perceive oneself as a robot" and that, conversely, "to learn the robot is to learn Buddhism." Paraphrasing the thirteenth-century Sōtō Zen master Dōgen, he noted, "To learn the Buddhist way is to learn about oneself. To learn about oneself is to forget oneself. To forget oneself is to perceive oneself as all things. To realize this is to cast off the body and mind of self and others."

As Mori writes in *The Buddha in the Robot*, "ignorance is seen in Buddhist philosophy as the fundamental cause of all evil."[122] Comparing humans to machines, he notes that humans are so complicated compared to other animals that not all their parts are synchronized properly. Therefore, he writes, using two Sanskrit terms directly transliterated (not translated) in Xuanzang's version of the Heart Sutra,

> If all human beings were running on all thousand
> wheels, the possibilities for the future would be
> infinite. The wisdom that we would have then would
> be what is spoken of in Buddhism as *prajñā*. We would
> have that unsurpassed enlightenment known as
> *anuttarā-samyak-saṃbodhi*.[123]

The year after I met him, Mori assumed the chairmanship of the Robotics Society of Japan and wrote to the members, emphasizing what are arguably the most important four Chinese characters in the entire Heart Sutra—色即是空:

> In Eastern philosophy we often use the famous
> phrase "form is indeed emptiness; emptiness is
> indeed form." Yet form is created from emptiness....
> A robot has form ... but it is also infinite. The robot's
> shape, the work it does, and the ways in which the

robot is applied are all infinite, just as life itself is infinite. Our Eastern philosophy is hinting to us that if we refine our insights and creativity, we can create limitless robots that are both interesting and useful. In other words, robot research and production can become a far greater source of spiritual enjoyment.[124]

Around the same time that I interviewed Mori, I also visited a "think tank" that he had founded in 1970. It was designed to promote creative thinking and came to be called the Jizai Institute. In vernacular Japanese *jizai* can mean "free or unrestricted." Only later did Mori realize that *jizai* was actually also a Buddhist term—with a somewhat similar meaning—and that it used the same Chinese characters as the second and third characters of "Avalokiteśvara," the name of the god/ess of mercy and narrator in the Xuanzang version of the Heart Sutra. It was only then, Mori says, that he became intensely interested in Buddhism and—while himself not a priest—eventually became a much sought-after lecturer and writer on the subject.

The Heart Sutra became my deep, deep connection to Buddhism. It may seem silly, but when gargling in the morning, when affixing my chop to documents, when driving the car and about to totally lose it, I would start chanting *kanjizai bosatsu gyōjin hannya-haramita*. If the phone rang when I was chanting the sutra at home, my first-grade daughter would pick it up and say, "Papa's doing that "*gyate gyate*" [mantra] stuff right now so call back later, okay?"[125]

At the time I visited Mori's think tank, it was also known in English as the Mukta Institute, *mukta* being the Sanskrit word for "freedom, liberation, and abandonment," devoid of Western connotations of libertinism and individualism. For over forty years member-clients of Mukta included executives at some of Japan's top corporations, such as Honda Motors, who would gather to study Buddhism, creativity, and read and chant sutras. And they especially chanted the Heart Sutra. As Matsubara Sueo—the head of a Tokyo robotics company and then acting president of Mukta—told me with a chuckle, "You really can't make a good robot without chanting the scriptures."[126]

Buddhism aside, Mori may be most famous today for a concept he introduced in 1970. In a provocative essay titled "Bukimi no tani," or "The Uncanny Valley," he questioned the wisdom of making robots too lifelike and illustrated his theory with a rising graph that has a sharp valley-like dip in the middle before rising again. Going up what might be called the "affinity" curve, as machines become more identifiably lifelike we feel closer to them, but just before a robot becomes a near-perfect replica of man, at the stage of wax dolls or android machines, the level of familiarity plunges and changes to a sense of the uncanny. Mori is cautioning future roboticists to avoid having their designs fall into this "Uncanny Valley" because humans will always feel closer to a robot slightly different from man and a little more "robot"-like.[127]

THE HEART SUTRA ROBOT

Thirty-three years after meeting Professor Mori, I went to see a "Heart Sutra robot" at the four-hundred-year-old Kōdai-ji temple complex in Kyoto, part of the Rinzai sect of Zen

Buddhism. Mori had no connection to the robot itself, but in several surprising ways it seemed to illustrate his theories. At the temple, Avalokiteśvara—known as Kannon, the Goddess of Compassion, in Japan and the "narrator" in the Heart Sutra—was displayed in an intimate-sized hall on the sprawling temple grounds. As a pamphlet said,

> Avalokiteśvara is the Bodhisattva of compassion and salvation, and can change into a variety of shapes for those seeking help. Today, in a world of technological development and increased psychological and material well-being, Avalokiteśvara has been revealed on the grounds of Kyoto's Kōdai-ji temple as the "Android Kannon MINDAR," for the many people who are still suffering.

Robots reciting the Heart Sutra are not entirely new. In 2011, in China, the Beijing Longquan Monastery developed a monk-robot, called Xian'er, that can recite sutras (including the Heart Sutra) and even answer simple questions. It became popular partly because it is designed to be cute and cartoonish; the monastery also created a cartoon strip and flash animations for the Xian'er character.[128] The Kōdai-ji MINDAR robot exists on an entirely different spiritual plane. It was not designed to be a cartoon, or a cartoon monk but to be a modern Bodhisattva statue that can be worshiped. And that is where Professor Mori's Uncanny Valley comes into play.

When I visited Kōdai-ji, I found that the MINDAR robot's head and hands were indeed android in appearance, covered with a highly realistic skin and looking entirely human. Yet in

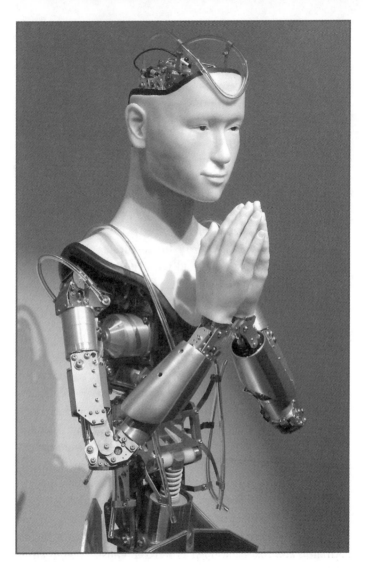

The Kōdai-ji MINDAR robot.

a seeming concession to Mori's theory of the Uncanny Valley, the robot's arms and chest were skeletal, with servo motors and wires all exposed. The lower torso was only represented abstractly, as the robot is stationary and does not move about the hall; it only moves its head, face, hands, and upper torso to a limited extent. The head was hairless and the face—the most detailed aspect of the robot—had eyes that blinked and moved and seemed uncannily real. But the aura the robot exuded was gender fluid. As the woman who presented the "show" noted, after cautioning everyone in the room to turn off their cell phones, this gender neutral look was appropriate, as the robot was supposed to approximate Avalokiteśvara, a Bodhisattva who can appear as male or female (or even an animal or something inanimate) depending on the viewer and who can travel through time and space.

After a short introduction, the show started. The robot's hands moved about in the air, but in a simplified way, in the sense that the fingers were not articulated; when the robot put his/her hands together, as if in prayer, they looked most realistic. The tone of speech was pleasant, and natural, with only a slight machine quality to it. Japanese speech is normally highly gender-specific, but this voice seemed gender-neutral, perhaps because, while the robot head itself looked vaguely feminine, it spoke matter-of-factly, like a Japanese male. Facial expressions and movements closely corresponded to the language used.

The show lasted about twenty-five minutes. As the robot spoke, images were projected on the wall behind, showing both abstract, cosmic scenes, as well as realistic scenes from nature, calligraphic images of the Xuanzang Heart Sutra itself, and even scenes of a virtual audience. Instead of merely reciting the Heart Sutra, the robot focused on an explanation of its enigmatic *kū* or "emptiness" concept. In response, members of the virtual human audience projected on the wall—who struggled to understand the seeming contradictions of "emptiness"—posed probing questions. The robot, in the role of a celestial Bodhisattva—in this case a Kannon or god/dess of mercy—gave explanations. No fancy AI or facial recognition technologies were employed to react with the real audience in the room. The robot was giving a repeatable, programmable sermon on the Heart Sutra and, for any non-Japanese in the audience, projection mapping provided English and Chinese translations on the wall.

There are said to be nearly eighty thousand Buddhist temples in Japan today, most with multiple, even dozens of Buddha statues or icons. The most revered statues tend to be old, even ancient, and almost always hand-made by humans. New ones usually go through a ceremony called a *kaigenshiki*, or "eye-opening," a consecration that imparts the Buddha nature to the statue. In the case of the Kōdai-ji Heart Sutra robot, one writer who attended the eye-opening—a vice priest from another sect, the Jōdo sect—wondered after seeing the robot whether anything could be a Buddha statue or object worthy of worship, even, for example, a Gundam Mobile Suit plastic model or a teddy bear? Since the MINDAR robot had been consecrated according to protocol (by a bevy of monks) and people in the audience seemed to worship it and pray and clasp their hands before it—in other words to entrust their faith in it—he came to the conclusion that it was working, resonating with the Buddha-nature in the viewers and therefore indeed legitimate.[129]

There were clearly technological and artistic challenges in creating the robot and its installation (which reportedly cost the temple nearly a million dollars). Not the least of these was finessing the Uncanny Valley curve, made extra-complicated because, while quasi-human in form, as an amorphous deity and object of worship this robot was not supposed to look *too* human in the first place.

The design of the physical robot was officially credited to Professor Ishiguro Hiroshi of Osaka University's Intelligent Robotics Lab, who is famous for his lifelike android creations. But most of the actual work was apparently done by Associate Professor Ogawa Kōhei, now of Nagoya University's Intelligent Systems group. In my view they succeeded remarkably well, and the "trick," Ogawa told me, may have been in not trying to make a completely humanoid robot (which would be impossible with today's technology), but to leave critical elements to the viewers' imagination for them to fill in on their own—for example to make the robot look gender-neutral by casting the chest portions somewhat masculine but the waist somewhat feminine, thus encouraging viewers to make their own assessment.[130] But they were also targeting a largely Japanese audience, presumably steeped since childhood in Buddhism, animism, and friendly robots from popular culture. In a *Chūnichi* newspaper article after the robot was revealed to the public, Kotō Tenshō—a high-ranking priest long affiliated with Kōdai-ji and the man considered to have given birth to the project—was quoted as saying, "Many people from abroad seem to have a negative impression because they imagine Frankenstein when they hear the word 'android.' But to us, who grew up with the likes of *Gigantor* and *Astro Boy*, a robot is something you can relate to like a friend."[131]

Writing the robot's sermon may have been even more difficult than designing the robot. At the temple I met one of a team of three scenario writers who worked on it, a Rinzai sect priest named Honda Dōryū. He later told me that they particularly struggled with two things. The first was the sutra's always-difficult but key concept of "emptiness." They had originally intended to focus on that in a faithful, easy-to-understand format, but this did not work because of its complexity and the fact that the compressed sutra itself does not expressly detail the benefits that a true understanding of emptiness can create in believers. They therefore had the android focus on how an understanding of the sutra can bring about compassion.

The second issue was how to justify using an android robot for the sermon, since sermons are normally given by human priests. The solution was to have a dialog with the virtual audience, led by the robot, that encouraged the real audience to think about what it means to be human and about the difference between robots and humans—to think about what humans have that robots don't. One solution, Honda says, was to concentrate on what is in Japanese called *bonnō* (煩悩, from the Sanskrit *kleśa*), the mental defilements such as greed, hatred, delusion, and other destructive states of mind that cause suffering, for which we humans seem to have an infinite capacity. As he put it, "By understanding the concept of emptiness we can empathize with others' emotions and grow closer to them. We can wish for their happiness, and as a result we ourselves can become happy."[132]

Signaling the success and interest in this project, the temple created a manga for those who want more information.

Titled (in translation) "An Android Kannon Talks about the Heart Sutra," it was supervised by four priests, including the aforementioned Honda. The story features three ordinary people suffering from a variety of modern and existential Japanese problems (a young university student trying to figure out his future; a middle aged man overworked by his company and burdened with debts at home; and an aging woman who discovers that she really doesn't like living with her husband when he retires). The three then visit Kōdai-ji, where the android robot gives them a sermon about the Heart Sutra—the "essence of Buddhism." The manga sermon loosely follows the real sermon at Kōdai-ji. In the manga, the android expounds on "emptiness" and the illusory and transitory nature of what we perceive as reality. S/he explains the need for us to see things as they really are, without interpreting them through the filter called "self," and also discusses the "wisdom" or "truth" in the sutra that can help free us from the sufferings of birth, sickness, aging, and death—and finally, how chanting the Heart Sutra mantra can help us find relief and peace. The manga book retails for the equivalent of about $10 and is sold at the temple and Amazon Japan as well as at numerous other sites. It has a short history of Xuanzang, essays on the robot and why it was created, a copy of the Xuanzang version of the Heart Sutra (with Japanese pronunciation keys), and a simple explanation of its meaning in modern Japanese.[133]

MODERN APPLICATIONS

If the application of the Heart Sutra to robotics seems counterintuitive, consider the world of fiction and drama, and even sports. In his 1996 book *Elaborations on Emptiness: Uses of the*

Heart Sutra, Professor Donald S. Lopez Jr., a Tibetan Buddhism expert, examines classical religious commentaries made on the sutra, its interpretations, and uses. He opens his book with a description of the now-famous "Story of Mimi-nashi Hōichi" (literally, "Hōichi-the-Earless").[134] In this tale, set centuries ago, a blind *biwa* lute player named Hōichi, who is staying at a Buddhist temple, is threatened by some vengeful ghosts from one of Japan's most spectacular and famous battles of the past. To protect him, the temple's priest and his acolyte use brush and ink to write the characters of the Heart Sutra all over his body, including the soles of his feet, but they forget to write it on his ears. When the vengeful ghosts return, they tear off Hōichi's ears, hence the title of the story.

This story was written by Lafcadio Hearn and included in his book *Kwaidan: Stories and Studies of Strange Things,* first published in 1904. Hearn (1850–1904), of Greek and Irish descent, had immigrated to the United States at nineteen and worked as a correspondent and writer, developing a popular writing style focused on clever observations of the often-exotic people and cultures around him. In 1890 he moved to Japan, grew enamored of already-fading traditional Japanese culture, married a Japanese woman, and became a Japanese citizen. He took the name Koizumi Yakumo and found his footing writing articles and books about old Japan for curious American and European audiences—to whom Japan was still an exotic culture about which they hungered to know more. Hearn never really learned to speak or read Japanese, but his writings about Japan, especially Japanese legends and ghost tales, became immensely popular in the West and even Japan.

"The Story of Mimi-nashi Hōichi" was based on a Japanese

tale that Hearn had heard and adapted liberally. Of the Heart Sutra, his knowledge came directly from F. Max Müller, one of the earliest scholars of the sutra, who had published a translation in 1881. Hearn did not quote the sutra in his story, only mentioning its Japanese name, *Hannya haramita shingyō*. But in an extensive footnote he explained that the Japanese name is a transliteration of the Sanskrit *Prajñāpāramitā Hṛdaya*. And he included what arguably was one of the first accessible, non-academic descriptions of the sutra in English to legions of his fans back in America:

> Apropos of the magical use of the text, as described in this story, it is worth remarking that the subject of the sutra is the Doctrine of the Emptiness of Forms,— that is to say, of the unreal character of all phenomena or noumena.... "Form is emptiness; and emptiness is form. Emptiness is not different from form; form is not different from emptiness. What is form — that is emptiness. What is emptiness—that is form.... Perception, name, concept, and knowledge, are also emptiness.... There is no eye, ear, nose, tongue, body, and mind.... But when the envelopment of consciousness has been annihilated, then he [*the seeker*] becomes free from all fear, and beyond the reach of change, enjoying final Nirvâna."[135]

Reality often imitates fiction and—taking inspiration from the story revived by Hearn—in 1995 a Japanese professional wrestler called Hakushi (ring name of Shinzaki Kensuke) began working in World Wrestling Entertainment matches in the

United States. He was famous for the Heart Sutra characters he had pasted or drawn all over his body and that he would enter the ring with to confront and, he hoped, terrify his opponents. As the WWE website featuring wrestling superstars notes, "Hakushi cut an impressive figure in an all-white ceremonial Japanese dress. But when he removed his conical hat and delicate robes to reveal a body that was covered from head to toe in Japanese script, he made an impression that few WWE fans would forget.... The ghostly Superstar left WWE in 1996 after being whacked by JBL with a branding iron."[136] No direct causality can be proved, but in photos he does not appear to have written the Heart Sutra on his ears.

HEART SUTRA BOOKS

In Japan's national library catalog, there are over one thousand five hundred books with the Chinese characters for "Heart Sutra" in the title, with new ones appearing every year, if not every month. When I visit Tokyo I always make it a point to visit major bookstores and look at the latest ones. Larger bookstores have sections on religion and specifically on Buddhism or Shinto and on the doctrinal teachings of various sects and cults, even on specific sutras. Even the imported "mindfulness" concept, pronounced as *maindofuruness*, has a rapidly growing section, which is today blurring into the Buddhist section, especially with books on Buddhism heavily influenced by Western interpretations or what even might be called "*katakana* Buddhism," from the word for the angular script used to indicate foreign words. But nothing compares to books on the Heart Sutra. Usually in their own marked area, they may occupy multiple shelves and cover nearly every possible use and interpretation of the sutra. Some describe how to do improved sutra copying, how to chant the sutra, or how to interpret it on a doctrinal basis according to various Buddhist sects. There are books about famous ancient commentaries on the Heart Sutra, new modern translations, translations of English works by Tibetan and Vietnamese masters, sophisticated history books, academic and nonacademic books, serious books, crackpot books making far-fetched claims, and parody humor books.

Representative of the last category is a 2016 book on the Heart Sutra with photos of a cute Japanese Shiba dog named Maru who, according to Amazon Japan, had 2.5 million followers on Instagram. As the book blurb says (translated), "You can learn about the Heart Sutra while enjoying cute photos, in a book chock-full of ways to become happy." Japanese for the Heart Sutra is *Hannya shingyō*, but in the book's title—*Shiba-ken Maru no WANnya shingyō*—there is a pun, with *Wan*, the Japanese sound of "Arf," substituted for the first character in *hannya* (般若, a Chinese/Japanese transliteration of the Sanskrit *prajñā*). I first found this book on sale at the sutra-copying hall of one of the most famous and sacred Heart Sutra–related temples in all of Japan—Yakushi-ji, in Nara, where—should we be surprised?—there were also copies of a cat version for sale.

Titles (in translation) of other books that have caught my eye in stores in recent years include:

The Heart Sutra for Cancer Patients
The Heart Sutra for Those With Depression
The Heart Sutra for Women
Heart Sutra: The Code Cracked, 2,000 Years of Silence Broken

Let's Try Writing the Heart Sutra in Sanskrit
Heart Sutra: Within the Limits of Reason, from the
Perspective of Ludwig Wittgenstein
Sutras to Dramatically Improve Your Luck
Heart Sutra Brain-Drills through Sutra-Copying
Healthy Heart Sutra Copying to Boost the Body's Immunity,
as Recommended by a Physician
The Heart Sutra, Newly Translated by a Writer Who Saw
the Other Side in a Near-Death Experience
The Heart Sutra, for Relaxation
The Rock and Roll Heart Sutra, Starting from Age
Twenty-Nine
The Heart Sutra, Explained by a Christian Minister

Looking beyond books to include newspaper and magazine articles, the vast range of modern Heart Sutra applications in Japan becomes even more apparent. There are clinical studies being done that seem to validate the benefits of sutra-copying, in particular, for brain health. And of course, there are dubious uses of the Heart Sutra, too. At the end of 2016, a member of the ruling Liberal Democratic Party made the news when, during deliberations in the National Diet on the merits of legalizing casinos, he used up his allotted time by simply reciting and explaining the Heart Sutra.[137]

What at first glance is simple and lighthearted can turn out to be surprisingly creative and useful. For example, many manga books, such as those by Kuwata Jirō, today explain the Heart Sutra to ordinary people. Kuwata is best known as the artist for the 1960s hit *8 Man*, a story about a hero robot-cop that became a globally popular TV anime series. After achieving

Heart Sutra section of a Tokyo bookstore.

huge initial success Kuwata had to navigate various personal issues, including divorces, an arrest, and time served for violating Japan's strict Firearms and Swords Control Act. Around 1985 he withdrew from the ordinary manga world (and largely from public life) and began drawing manga about religion and spiritual subjects. Kuwata passed away in 2020, but in his lifetime authored nearly twenty popular books about the Heart Sutra, one even specifically on the "emptiness" theory within it.

One of the more interesting works on the Heart Sutra in recent years in Japan is a non-manga created in 2007 by a famous manga artist, Miura Jun, a close friend of the abbot at Sumidera temple in Kyoto mentioned in chapter 7. Miura's Heart Sutra book is not a manga but an art photobook, compiled from five years of studying the sutra and traveling around Japan, taking pictures of public signs and billboards—all written in different styles—that contain the individual Chinese characters that appear in the Xuanzang version of the Heart Sutra and then adding his own poignant comments and observations. Given that several of the characters in the Heart Sutra are rarely used in Japan today, he had to struggle mightily to find some of them. In this sense, his work is like the sixth-century stone Heart Sutra stele described in chapter 6, which took the monk Huairen over two decades to inscribe using the calligraphic style of the long-departed master Wang Xizhi. Appropriately, Miura's work is titled *Autodoa Hannya shingyō*—"Outdoor Heart Sutra"—reflecting his long hours searching outside. As Miura writes, in a blend of humor and seriousness (translated),

> "Sutra-copying" of the Heart Sutra is very popular. By focusing the mind, by writing the sutra text over and over again, it enables the sutra-copier to enter a state of "nothingness." Ultimately, what seems to get in the way of "nothingness" is one's own "self."... Instead of sutra-copying, this book is about sutra-photograph-copying.... When I came up with this idea, I thought it would be easy to find the images I needed, but oh how difficult it was.... I nearly gave up many times, but it is true that my burning desire to finish this project at least for a

second put me in a state of "nothingness." And the project also worked like a diet for me, too.[138]

The demand for popular books on the Heart Sutra is stimulated by intense curiosity—which is in turn generated by the inherent complexity of the ideas in the short and seemingly simple sutra itself. And it is also generated by language. In Korea, and also Vietnam, where the Xuanzang version of the Heart Sutra was once written in its original format with Chinese characters, most people today read it in their native language. This is because Chinese characters have largely been abandoned in daily life as new phonetic scripts or alphabets have been adopted in standardized new writing systems. In Japan, China, and much of the Chinese diaspora, however, it is still possible to learn to read the Xuanzang version of the sutra in *exactly* the same visual format in which it was presented 1,400 years ago, thereby gleaning some sort-of-maybe understanding. This tenuous connection can be immensely furthered with only a little bit of study—perhaps only a little more effort than modern English speakers have to make to read Chaucer's fourteenth-century Middle English. And this often kindles a deep desire to read more about the ancient sutra, to read what ancient Chinese and Japanese sages have said, as well as what modern secular and religious thinkers have to say about its often opaque and hidden meanings.

The difficulty of understanding some terms in the sutra today was driven home to me in a somewhat humorous way by the work of the famous artist Ikeda Masuo (1934–97). Ikeda had great notoriety in 1960s and '70s Japan for his modern, multimedia art, often highly charged with eroticism. My personal, though very oblique, connection to him comes from a lovely stray dog that long ago adopted me in Tokyo, to my dismay (since I could not keep her), until Ikeda's first ex-wife adopted her. In 2018, when I visited the Paramita Museum in Mie Prefecture, I was astounded to find an enormous and diverse ceramic installation of Ikeda's, titled "Heart Sutra," since I had never heard of his religious leanings (or, since he is best known for his prints, even much about his ceramics). A deluxe book published by the museum about the exhibit has lavish photographs of the ceramics, essays on Ikeda and how he created his work, and of course a copy of the Heart Sutra itself. Ikeda himself also penned an article titled (translated) "The Heart Sutra: Emptiness and Nothingness," and in it he describes his feelings when originally commissioned to do the installation. At first, he says, he turned the request down because he felt that he didn't know enough about either the sutra or even Buddhism. And even though he read as many books as he could, he struggled with the sutra's abstract concepts of "emptiness and form" and "emptiness and nothingness."

> Most Japanese, even if they don't know any other sutras, know about the Heart Sutra, even if their knowledge of it is completely shallow. Even if they can't recite the sutra by heart, nearly everyone remembers the phrase 色即是空, the *shiki-soku-ze-kū*, or "form is indeed emptiness." That's exactly the way I was. And while I'm embarrassed to admit it, like ordinary people, I associated the first character, 色, with the same first character in the compound 色欲 [*shiki-yoku*], meaning lust or sexual appetite.[139]

A SEARCH FOR UNDERSTANDING

Many people assert that it takes years of study or meditation to understand the Heart Sutra, in particular its emptiness theory. There is no lack of books that purport to explain emptiness and the core phrase in the Heart Sutra, stating that "form is no different from emptiness; emptiness is no different from form; form is indeed emptiness, emptiness is indeed form." Entire forests may have been felled to do so. Not surprisingly, many of these books can appall serious academics and religious figures, who have often spent long years seriously studying and contemplating the sutra.

Harada Wasō, priest and author of the aforementioned 446-page treatise on the Heart Sutra, is a good example. In his introduction, he says,

> [A]n enormous number of explanatory books have been written about the Heart Sutra by people in a wide variety of industries, including priests, writers, businessmen, scientists, and so forth. Most of them have used the Heart Sutra text to pour out their own understanding of Buddhism and contributed shockingly little to an actual understanding of the sutra.... In terms of clarifying the Heart Sutra itself, what seems to support the mass production of these barren "explanatory" books is the fact that writers, readers, and publishers share the baseless fantasy or delusion (indeed, the 顛倒夢想 [or "distortion and delusions"] mentioned in the sutra) that anyone with a little grounding in Buddhism can decipher the Heart Sutra.[140]

The late Fukui Fumimasa (Bunga), high priest of the Tendai sect and doyen of Japan's serious writing on the Heart Sutra, is almost apoplectic on this subject, especially when considering popular definitions of "emptiness" (or what is written in Chinese characters as 空). In his 2008 book, he includes a blistering critique of existing explanations and by extension modern Japanese society—the sort of critique in Japan only someone of his age and status can easily deliver. Most definitions, he says, even he doesn't understand. On reading the definition of "emptiness" in the *Kōjien*, one of Japan's most prestigious dictionaries, he notes that it was created by a man (presumably Nakamura Hajime, who was then Japan's leading authority on Indian philosophy) using fancy words like 実態 ("substance") that sound as if they had been borrowed from the eighteenth-century German philosopher Immanuel Kant:

> No one will ever say or write that they can't understand it. And if you say the wrong thing, it's almost as though you'll be yelled at by his followers, saying, "if you don't understand, it just shows you're stupid and need to study more, until you do understand." It's a negative example of the authoritarianism and academic factionalism that leads people in Japan to always say "yes, yes" in agreement to whatever a famous teacher says, whether they really agree or not.

Never too reticent, Fukui offers readers his own easier-to-understand definition by using an analogy contrasting "emptiness" with "nothingness." An "empty seat," he says, means that there is a seat, but that the person who should be sitting there is not present. "No seat" means that the seat never existed. When a person arrives, the seat functions as a seat because of the force, function, and connections of its 縁 or "conditions," and this is what is meant by the Buddhist term, 縁起 or "dependent arising.[141]

Thanks to Buddha, and the ancients, the Heart Sutra and the emptiness concept can have infinite usefulness, even today. Yet perhaps it was Edward Conze, the great twentieth-century scholar of Prajñāpāramitā sutras, who in 1948 best summed up the core problem that modern "explainers" of the Heart Sutra also face:

> The *Prajñāpāramitā* texts are so elusive to our understanding, because they are full of hidden hints, allusions, and indirect references to the pre-existing body of scriptures and traditions circulating in the memory of the Buddhist community at the time. They are more often than not an echo of older sayings. Without the relation to the older sayings they lose most of their point. We at present have to reconstruct laboriously what seemed a matter of course 1,500 years ago.[142]

New Life in a New World

The quest to determine the Heart Sutra's original meaning often leads academics to study classical Chinese, Sanskrit, or Tibetan. And in modern Japan it sometimes leads ordinary people to read Japanese translations of books originally in English by Tibetan, Vietnamese, and other masters—occasionally even to read English translations of the Xuanzang version of the sutra itself. On one of my periodic trips to the Heart Sutra shelves of major Tokyo bookstores, I was amused to see a 2013 book by writer/TV personality/English expert Takemura Hideo, titled (in loose translation), "The Heart Sutra Is Easier to Understand in English." He had chapters on specific elements of the sutra, including the "emptiness is none other than form" section and the mantra, explaining in Japanese how they are explained in English. The target market for such books in Japan, presumably, is the millions of people interested in Buddhism and especially the Heart Sutra who want to know how the sutra is expressed in a vastly different language like English. Some particularly undaunted readers, perhaps unaware of the enormity of the challenge, may even be hoping to improve their English skills along the way.

The lotus, a Buddhist symbol of enlightenment blooming over the material world.

There is a certain logic in believing that English translations of Xuanzang's ancient version of the sutra are easier to understand. They are all inherently a newer, more modern interpretation of a nearly 1,400-year-old-work, the original of which Chinese and Japanese today can only read with effort. And modern English can be far more precise than ordinary Japanese and Chinese, since in English subjects and objects and singulars and plurals often *have* to be specified. Conversely, in modern translations there is always a risk in specifying what may originally have been deliberately written as nonspecific, and in the process even introducing more confusion. The "precision" might be misleading.

Should a translation try to preserve the eloquence and brevity of the Xuanzang version? Should it reference Sanskrit,

Tibetan, Uyghur, Mongolian, and Chinese versions, or just the Chinese? Should it also be easy to chant? Should it be poetic? Or should it just concentrate on conveying meaning? Until recently many translators seemed to base their work on the Xuanzang Chinese version but would also reference the Sanskrit version, perhaps to add an aura of authenticity, especially if asserting that Xuanzang's version had been translated from a Sanskrit original in India.

An ambitious project undertaken in Japan around 1990 to create a "standard" or "canonical" English translation—one that could be used globally—illustrates some of the complicated issues translators confront. Nanba Mitsusada, best known as the abbot of the Jōdo sect's Seirin-ji temple in Tokyo, formed a team to carry out his goal of helping the people of the world develop "a gentle spirit." Writing in 2010, in an article titled (translated) "An English Translation of the Heart Sutra: It's So Easy to Understand in English," he says he chose the Heart Sutra as something with which all Japanese are familiar and because it is "a critical Buddhist sutra that condenses the essence of all of Buddha's teachings into a mere 262 characters ... and also because from ancient times it has been believed to be an incantation that protects people from misfortune." Eventually, the team's translation was rendered into Braille, French, Coptic, Syrian languages, and ancient Greek.[143]

Nanba put together a team made up of the award-winning American-born novelist, critic, and translator Levy Hideo (now a naturalized Japanese) as well as Buddhologists, monks, English experts, and religion journalists. The team held regular meetings to discuss translation issues and, while working from Xuanzang's version of the sutra, also referenced Sanskrit texts. Levy originally translated the mantra portion of the sutra into English as "Gone, gone across, you who have gone across, across to the other shore, you who have reached the other shore. Blessed be wisdom," but after endless debates the team convinced him to use the original Sanskrit sound, or *Gaté gaté pāragaté pārasaṃgaté bodhi svāhā*, because that is what Xuanzang had used.

As one would expect, the result of the project's translation is similar to the multitudes of other translations (almost all of which reference Edward Conze or D. T. Suzuki's earlier works). But perhaps because Buddhist scholars were involved, the team made attempts to unpack some of the references embedded in Xuanzang's Chinese. For example, what Xuanzang had expressed in a mere nine characters—無限界乃至 無意識界—becomes quite different. D. T. Suzuki translated this in 1934 as "no Dhatu of vision, till we come to no Dhatu of consciousness."[144] Edward Conze translated it in 1956 as "No sight-organ element, and so forth, until we come to: No mind-consciousness element."[145] And in 1988, Thich Nhat Hanh, the famous Vietnamese Buddhist master, translated it simply as "No realms of elements (from eyes to mind-consciousness)."[146] In the 1990 Nanba version, however, it becomes "There are no eighteen realms from 'there is no realm of eyes' to 'there is no realm conceived by mind.'" In other words, because Buddhism has an abundance of nested lists, it is possible to unpack lines of Xuanzang's Chinese to bring out the "twelve-linked causes of pain" and "four truths," which Xuanzang does not explicitly state in Chinese; nor, for that matter, do most modern English translations. One exception is Thich Nhat Hanh, who in 2014 went back and revised his original translation, unpacking phrases to include the "Eighteen Realms of Phenomena," "the six Sense Organs," "the six Sense Objects," and "the six Consciousnesses," as well as the "Twelve Links of Interdependent Arising."[147]

Unpacking hidden meanings is helpful for those trying to understand the Buddhist context of the sutra, but putting the explanation in the body of the sutra instead of in footnotes, sidenotes, or endnotes creates a different set of difficulties. Since Buddhism has so many sublists nested in lists, once a translator unpacks one implied numbered list (such as the eighteen realms) from a few Chinese characters in Xuanzang's version, it puts quite a burden on readers, not to mention chanters, and makes liturgical use of the sutra even more complicated. In our modern digital world, this would be an ideal place to exploit hypertext links to allow readers to drill down on ancient meanings and trace them back to their heart's content.

Since modern language is constantly evolving, contemporary translators also have to consider the impermanence of the words they use to represent Xuanzang's characters. D. T. Suzuki's 1934 translation of the Heart Sutra remains one of the gold standards in the English world, but he translated the Sino-Japanese character 行 (from the Sanskrit word *saṃskāra*) as "confections." *Saṃskāra* is an admittedly difficult word whose meaning morphs according to context (it is often said to mean "activity," "formations," or even "karmic predispositions"). While "confection" may have worked when Suzuki used it in 1934, for modern readers it is more likely to evoke images of sweet pastries.

There is an even bigger problem when rendering Xuanzang's text into modern languages. Once the Heart Sutra is translated into something outside of the Sino-Japanese cultural orbit (where Xuanzang's text is still readable), the "master" version is lost. There are surely hundreds of modern translators of the Heart Sutra now, if one includes famous religious figures and aspiring religious figures, academics, and sutra aficionados. And if each one chooses different terms, the underlying unity of the master sutra is lost and a sense of shared connectivity among practitioners is weakened. One such result is that in North America and Europe, where Buddhism has grown dramatically in the last century, different sects use different versions, whether chanting or meditating or contemplating. And every translation group (or individual) probably hopes their version will be the purest, or even become a universal standard. The Taiwan-based Fo Guang Shan, with centers around the world, has its own translation. So, too, does the Dharma Realm Buddhist Association, which maintains the City of Ten Thousand Buddhas in Ukiah, California, and numerous branches elsewhere. So, too, do Sōtō and Rinzai Zen sect branches in the Americas and Europe.

When it comes to chanting the Heart Sutra, Chinese, Korean, Vietnamese, Japanese, or Tibetan immigrant communities outside of East Asia may still use their native languages. But at other temples—especially those of Zen sects—that often attract more European Americans, the chanting is usually done in English or the language of the constituents. Occasionally, devotees overseas may even prefer to chant the Heart Sutra in Chinese or Japanese, even if they have no comprehension of the language at all. This may be especially true of esoteric sects, such as the Japanese Koyasan Shingon, where more emphasis is placed on pure sound recitation. According to Daigaku

Rummé, longtime practitioner and priest of the Sōtō Zen sect, "in Europe, we see the tendency for Sōtō practitioners to chant the Heart Sutra in Japanese, but here in the United States it seems to be mostly chanted in English, although some places like the San Francisco Zen Center chant it both ways."[148]

THE HEART SUTRA IN ENGLISH

Outside Asia as in Asia itself, despite all these linguistic issues, the more people are exposed to the Heart Sutra, the more they want to know about it, to contemplate it, and to study it. Nearly all modern Buddhist figures with a global audience in the world, including luminaries like the Dalai Lama and Thich Nhat Hanh, have their own English translations, as well as extensive commentaries. There are also a growing number of translations of classic commentaries from ancient China and Japan and even India (via Tibet). These include texts by K'uei-chi (632–82), the most outstanding disciple of Xuanzang, and English translations of Tibetan translations of Sanskrit versions of Indian commentaries on the text (between the eighth and twelfth centuries), as well as English translations of Japanese commentaries by the famous Rinzai Zen master Hakuin Ekaku (1686–1769) and by the saint and founder of Shingon Buddhism, Kūkai (784–835).

And again, as in East Asia, the power of the Heart Sutra leads people in the West to discover new contexts for its message. In 2019, American Buddhologist Paula Arai authored a book titled *Painting Enlightenment: Healing Visions of the Heart Sutra* about the individualistic art of the Japanese scientist and devout Buddhist Iwasaki Tsuneo (1917–2002). Arai's book has arguably made Iwasaki better known in the United States than Japan, which, if past history is our guide, may lead back to his increased recognition in Japan. One of the publisher's blurbs for the book was written by Ruben L. F. Habito, whose byline itself—he is described as the author of *Healing Breath: Zen for Christians and Buddhists in a Wounded World*— reveals the breadth of Buddhist and Heart Sutra applications in the United States. Habito praises the expansiveness of Iwaskai's approach as follows:

> ... [Iwasaki] reveals to us a wondrous universe suf-
> fused with the light of the Buddha's enlightenment
> experience. He does so by embedding the characters
> of the Heart Sutra, a famous Mahayana scriptural
> text, in depictions of the macrocosmic Big Bang
> scene, of the microcosmic double helix in the DNA
> molecule structure, as well as of ordinary landscapes
> and natural scenery.... This is a breathtaking glimpse
> of our intimately interconnected universe.[149]

While Arai's book focuses on Iwasaki's art and includes her own extensive commentary, she also includes an English translation of the Heart Sutra by Kazuaki ("Kaz") Tanahashi and Joan Halifax, as well as a famous and poignant quote about the sutra by Kūkai—"The truth expressed in the [Heart] Sutra is everywhere to be seen: it is in our mind, the beginning and end of which are unknown."[150]

On a similar but even more direct metaphysical level, in 1991 Mu Soeng Sunim—an ordained monk in the Korean Zen tradition and a prolific American writer on Buddhism— authored a commentary titled *Heart Sutra: Ancient Buddhist*

A few Heart Sutra books in English.

Wisdom in the Light of Quantum Reality. In his introduction, Sunim (taking a cue from Fritjof Capra's groundbreaking 1975 book *The Tao of Physics*) writes, "Now that quantum physics has found some very interesting parallels to the basic insights of the *Heart Sutra*, perhaps the intellectual and the intuitive can meet in the new paradigm."[151] In 2010, he updated this book and added a new title, *The Heart of the Universe: Exploring the Heart Sutra,* and included his own brand-new translation—what he calls a playful and serious "free-form rendering" of the Heart Sutra.

SUTRA COPYING IN THE WEST

Given the cultural and linguistic barriers, it is hard to imagine sutra-copying in the West ever achieving the popularity it has in China and Japan, where there is a deeply rooted culture of calligraphy. Yet there is at least one book in English specifically about Heart Sutra calligraphy, by artist Nadja Van Ghelue, originally from Belgium. In 2009 she authored *The Heart Sutra in Calligraphy: A Visual Appreciation of the Perfection of Wisdom*, writing the Heart Sutra using calligraphy in what is known as "seal script" style. This script is a marvelously archaic Chinese style of writing characters that fell out of popularity hundreds of years before the birth of Christ and is today used mainly for decorative or limited official purposes (almost no one in Japan or China can easily read or write it anymore). For modern readers, Van Ghelue also includes the modern (Xuanzang era) characters for the sutra but gives their romanized pronunciation in Japanese, with an English translation. In her introduction she writes:

> As the word "religion" comes from the Latin *religare*, which means to bind or come together, we could thus state that art is actually a religious performance, born from a sense of reunion. As it binds, it allows us to go beyond the limits of the small self and expand to our big mind, which we could call Love, Original Mind, Buddha Mind, or Emptiness.... Copying the Heart Sutra has played an especially important role in my life, as its subject is precisely this original emptiness.[152]

A SUTRA WORTH STUDYING

In the summer of 1976 I walked from Tokyo to Kyoto on a trail over five hundred miles long, through fields and forests and over mountains and through deep valleys. I started with a Japanese friend who halfway through wore out his boots, and I finished alone, exhausted. For most of the trip I slept out in the open, but sometimes I stayed in Buddhist temples along the way. It was one of the highlights of my life, and toward the end, as I approached Kyoto, through mosquitoes and leeches and rains and howling typhoon weather, the rhythm of walking became almost trancelike, and I began chanting the Heart Sutra mantra—which was all I knew at the time—over and over.

After arriving in Kyoto, I happened to meet an old Tokyo high school friend, David Rummé. I hadn't seen him for years, but in our senior year at an international school both of us had lived in different dormitories (originally intended to house children of Christian missionaries, which he was but I was not), and our girlfriends had been good friends. David was tall (6' 5") and thin, described in the school yearbook as "lanky and dark" and, with a quote from Samuel Butler's *Hudibras*, as "a deep occult philosopher."

In Kyoto, after graduating from college in America, to my mind David looked like a modern Christ-figure, with long hair down to the middle of his back, but with a tie-dyed T-shirt. Over a bowl of noodles at Kyoto Station, he told me of his spiritual journey and his intention to enter a Sōtō Zen monastery in Japan, which he did. He became Daigaku—written with the characters for "big" and "mountain" or "peak"—Rummé, with a shaved head, and spent the next twenty-seven years meditating in what most people would consider extraordinarily rigorous conditions, being hospitalized for a year with TB along the way, his weight never exceeding 150 pounds. As I noted earlier, nearly every day his practice at the monastery involved chanting the Heart Sutra (as well as other sutras).

After his long and intensive training, Daigaku returned to the United States in 2003 where today, after serving as North America's first non-Japanese *sōkan*, or Director of the Association of Sōtō Zen Buddhists, equivalent to a bishop, he is the resident priest and teacher at the Confluence Zen Center in St. Louis, Missouri. Of the Heart Sutra, he says,

> Since it is said to be the kernel (or heart) of the Great Perfect Wisdom Sutra, and is often said to encapsulate the whole of the Buddhist teaching, I think it would be difficult for the Heart Sutra not to have a special meaning for someone who dedicates their life to Buddhist practice and realization. The question of emptiness and nothingness, for example, the statement "no eyes, ears, nose, etc."; the final *gatha* which we always heard said to be the words exclaimed by the Buddha at the time of his awakening, i.e. his guarantee that all beings are in the state of Buddhahood; and the end of suffering that Avalokiteśvara Bodhisattva experienced as a result of seeing into the emptiness of the body and mind—it's hard for me to imagine someone not being personally challenged by these teachings.[153]

Afterword

In the city of Kanazawa on the west coast of Japan's Honshu Island I once came across what I have ever since thought to be one of the best physical and artistic depictions of the phrase "form is not different from emptiness." It was at a museum dedicated to D. T. Suzuki, the great modern Zen thinker and proselytizer whose 1934 translation of the Heart Sutra heavily influenced curious minds in the West.

In a silent and meditative outdoor area was a beautiful rectangular expanse of water in a pool, whose surface was absolutely still. The stillness was only disturbed periodically by a randomly generated ripple that spread from a central point across the water's surface and then ever so gradually disappeared. Just before I exited the museum, I saw on a wall Suzuki's symbolic representation of the Heart Sutra phrase 色不異空, what he translates as "form is no other than emptiness." Inspired by a famous drawing by seventeenth-century Zen master Sengai, it consists of a brush painting presented in a Zen *kōan*-riddle style—a vertical array of a triangle overlaid on a square, the characters 不異 ("not-different"), and a circle. In English, Suzuki would apparently often explain this

D. T. Suzuki's *kōan* visualization of "Form is not different from emptiness."
Courtesy Suzuki Daisetsu Museum.

as representing the "universe," with all its infinite time and space. To me, it also seems to symbolize the need to avoid becoming too fixated on the etymology of words and to not try too hard to intellectualize the impossible.

In my own life, the Xuanzang version of the Heart Sutra resonates deeply, often for reasons I cannot explain verbally, leading me to believe that all interpretations are probably, ultimately, highly personal. Nonetheless, while I can claim no authority in religious matters, to me it has become sort of a religious North Star, something that will continue to fascinate and guide me forever, not only for its history but for the way it constantly challenges me, emotionally and intellectually.

I now find my own references to it, both direct and indirect, in surprising places. Often, they are very local, right in the San Francisco Bay Area where I live. Sometimes they are in a backyard garden statue of a sinewy Avalokiteśvara. Once it was on a wall in a traditional Japanese-style building in the otherwise secular Hakone Gardens in Saratoga, California, where an inscription hung of 色即是空, or "Form is indeed emptiness." Sometimes it is in Buddhist environments, such as the City of Ten Thousand Buddhas in Northern California, where I spotted a large incense burner used by monks with the entire Heart Sutra engraved on it, the exact same one as that used by the Fo Guang Shan sect in Taiwan. Sometimes it is graffiti in San Francisco or Oakland's Chinatown, where I have spotted Xuanzang-themed Journey to the West murals. And sometimes the references are mysterious and not at all visual.

Pre-pandemic, I used to play guitar and sing with a dear friend twice a month, as a volunteer at a memory care ward in San Francisco for people with Alzheimer's and other cognitive disorders. We started out playing old standards, but as time went by we realized the patients were younger than we thought, so we began occasionally including pop songs such as John Lennon's "Imagine." The more I played Lennon's song, the more the lyrics, replete with negatives, reminded me of the Heart Sutra. This puzzled me. But when Lennon's wife Yoko Ono (from Heart Sutra land) was granted co-songwriting credits in 2017, I noted that many Lennon fans in Japan were making a similar association. I also saw that on the Web there are even photographs (by Bob Gruen) of Yoko and John strolling about New York, John wearing a jacket with the left sleeve embroidered with 摩訶般若波羅蜜多心経, a common title given in Japan to Xuanzang's Heart Sutra. I have no idea if Lennon and Ono consciously thought about the Heart Sutra when composing the song's lyrics. But suddenly, as a listener, making the connection didn't seem so absurd after all.

On a more prosaic level, during the time I have been writing this book, I find myself surrounded by the Heart Sutra at home. I have Heart Sutra books galore in English, Japanese, and Chinese, as one might expect, but I also have Xuanzang Heart Sutra T-shirts, neckties, tea cups, fans, beads, CDs, amulets, necklaces, mala beads, calligraphy scrolls—and a ring that I wear on my left pinky finger with the entire sutra engraved so small I need a magnifying glass to read it. Not too long ago, I met with a priest from Japan's esoteric Koyasan Shingon sect of Buddhism. Having heard of my interest in the sutra, he gave me an example of the then-latest Heart Sutra paraphernalia from Japan—a ballpoint pen with a spring-wound copy of the entire sutra inside, with a slit in the side that allows it to be retracted and viewed as needed, before snapping back into the shaft. He couldn't have made me happier.

Of course, for me the Heart Sutra is far more than

paraphernalia. While writing this book I have studied the Xuanzang version over and over again, occasionally copying it, but more often chanting it. In the beginning, as outlined in the first chapter, I only knew the mantra portion. But I was deeply inspired by watching others, including my friend Yūhō, a longtime monk/priest, recite it as part of his daily routine at a Rinzai Zen temple in Kyoto. It took a while, but I finally memorized the entire sutra in Japanese pronunciation myself. I am at the point now where it runs through my brain regularly, and I can see the Sino-Japanese characters streaming by, almost like a chyron on a television screen.

Have I become enlightened? Far from it. As a typically weak human, I am sometimes the victim of neurotic thoughts and existential terror, unsolvable mental dilemmas, and occasionally even what might be called clinical depression in what often seems a broken world, a world full of wars and terror and cruelty and climate change and global pandemics. Yet reciting the sutra gives me focus, and despite what might be perceived as a string of negations in the "emptiness" portion of its text, at times it almost seems to cleanse my brain, my consciousness. The more turmoil my world seems to be engulfed in, the more peace it gives me.

On a purely intellectual level, I also find that the Heart Sutra's "emptiness theory" can function like the rudder on a ship. Everyone may have their own interpretation of it, but to me it is such a challenging notion that I will spend the rest of my life thinking about it. I will never become a daily *zazen* meditator, or even join a religious sect, but I will continue to contemplate the "emptiness" concept in the Heart Sutra and other Buddhist teachings. In a way, I find the Heart Sutra to be the ultimate existential and deconstruction tool, something that helps me step outside of myself and try to see the world as it really is, beyond the normal filters of my inherited physical body and its temporal limitations. If you believe that human arrogance is an issue in life, or if you believe, as I do, that a household pet or a tree outside may be just as smart (in its own way) as a human, or if you believe that suffering is all too common and that compassion can be a solution, then the Heart Sutra may also be useful for you, too. Although I completely failed to understand the emptiness theory in the beginning, I see now how it can lead to greater compassion for other beings.

At the beginning of this book, I mentioned how the Heart Sutra mantra helped me steady myself during an aborted plane flight. Before I finished this book, I was returning on a freeway from an interpreting job in Silicon Valley at dusk, in rush hour. A car suddenly plowed into my lane, sending my motorcycle and me on completely different vectors. When I staggered to my feet, my bike was directly behind me in the middle of the four or five lanes of the freeway, and behind it I could see a phalanx of cars mercifully stopped, their headlights glaring at me in the dark. Two Good Samaritans saved me by helping me to the side of the road and calling the California Highway Patrol and an ambulance, which took me to the emergency room with three ribs and a clavicle broken. I was intensely grateful for simply having survived against all odds, but when waves of pain and dizziness washed over me in the ambulance, I began to worry that my luck might have run out completely. I also worried that I might never finish this book. Then, once again mentally reciting the entire sutra, I found that it helped to stabilize my mind, to concentrate, to stay conscious, and to remind myself of the phrase embedded in the "emptiness" portion of the sutra, of 無有恐怖, of how, with no hindrances, "there is no fear." Later, an acquaintance in Japan who is an expert on the Heart Sutra wrote me to say that I was probably under the "protection of Buddha." Whether that is true or not, I do not know, but by the time my injuries had healed the global pandemic of 2020 had begun, accompanied by vast political and social instability—so much so that at times the entire earth seemed to have been shaken off its axis. And the Heart Sutra would again provide solace and a stability in the midst of even greater uncertainty—an uncertainty so vast and deep that my accident would come to seem almost laughably insignificant.

With a spirit of gratitude to Buddha and the ancients who bequeathed us such a wonderful sutra, upon turning in my manuscript I made another copy of the sutra and sent it to the Fo Guang Shan temple complex in Taiwan. It could have been any temple in the world that does this sort of thing, but at this particular one I had in the past purchased a special "sutra copying kit" that is provided to interested visitors (and may be obtained remotely from around the world). These kits include the proper sutra-copying paper and calligraphy pen. The copied sutras are annually collected as part of a "One Million Heart Sutras in the Buddha" program and then carried by scores of orange-robed monks up to the top of a giant stupa, where they not only help the calligraphers accumulate merit but are stored "as blessings in dedication to all beings."

FLS
San Francisco, California, 2020

Endnotes

1   Federal Aviation Administration, "Lessons Learned from Civil Aviation Accidents; Japan Airlines Flight 123, Boeing 747-Sr100, Ja8119: Accident Overview," https://lessonslearned.faa.gov/Japan123/JAL123_Acc_Report.pdf (accessed 17 December 17 2019).

2   From "Buddhism and The Beats" (Ginsberg 1993—I—Introduction), a documentary made by Robyn Brentano and the NYU Ethnographic Film Program, transcribed at http://allenginsberg.org/2017/07/s-j-15/ (accessed 13 March 2018).

3   Jack Kerouac, *Some of the Dharma* (New York: Viking, 1997). See "About the Manuscript" and p. 8.

4   Quotation from transcript of interview done at Commonwealth Club of California on 15 May 2002, listed on the biographical guide in the University of California, Davis, "Inventory of the Gary Snyder Papers." https://oac.cdlib.org/findaid/ark:/13030/tf1489n5dm/entire_text/.

5   Gary Snyder, *Turtle Island* (New York: New Directions, 1974), p. 66.

6   Alex Wayman et al., "Secret of the Heart Sutra," *Prajñaparamita and Related Systems* (1977): 308–9.

7   Dana Goodyear, "Zen Master: Gary Snyder and the Art of Life," *The New Yorker*, 20 October 2008: 66–75. Gary Snyder, "Walking the Great Ridge Omine on the Diamond-Womb Trail," *Kyoto*

Journal 25 (24 December 1993).

8   Allen Ginsberg, "The Vomit of a Mad Tyger," *Shambhala Sun.* 2, no. 6 (1994): 14–23, 54–59.

9   Ibid.

10 This rendition can be heard on the Internet Archive in a file titled "Anne Waldman and Allen Ginsberg lecture on dharma poetics, June, 1996" at approximately 1:08:50 into the talk. https://archive.org/details/Anne_Waldman_and_Allen_ Ginsberg_lecture__96P023 (accessed 14 April 2018).

11 Ginsberg can be heard performing the Heart Sutra with Clash on "Ghetto Defendant" in the 1982 CD *Combat Rock.*

12 In his book *A Brief History of China*, Jonathan Clements gives a description of the issues involved in assaying what sort of sound people might have given to ideograms 1,400 years ago: "Many ancient poems don't rhyme any more in modern Mandarin, having been garbled down the centuries.... Much as the best way to hear the English of the Dark Ages now requires a trip to Iceland, if you want to know what Chinese really sounded like in the Tang dynasty, you're better off eavesdropping on the streets of Guangzhou in the far south, or taking in a Sichuan opera. Jonathan Clements, *A Brief History of China: Dynasty, Revolution, and Transformation* (North Clarendon, VT: Tuttle Publishing, 2019), p. 13.

13 Oxford English Dictionary, *"Mantra, N.,"* 3rd ed. (Oxford: Oxford University Press, 2000).

14 Bstan-dzin-rgya-mtsho, Dalai Lama XIV, and Thupten Jinpa, *Essence of the Heart Sutra: The Dalai Lama's Heart of Wisdom Teachings* (Boston: Wisdom Publications, 2005), pp. 129–31.

15 T'an Hsu, *The Prajna Paramita Heart Sutra* (New York: Sutra Translation Committee of the U.S. and Canada, 2000), p. 21.

16 Samuel Beal, *A Catena of Buddhist Scriptures from the Chinese* (London: Trübner, 1871), pp. 279–84. "The Páramitá-Hṛidaya Sútra, or, in Chinese, 'Moho-pō-ye-po-lo-mih-to-sin-king,' i.e., 'The Great Páramitá Heart Sútra,'" *Journal of the Royal Asiatic Society of*

Great Britain and Ireland, New Series 1, no. 1/2 (1865): 28.

17 Friedrich Max Müller, *Buddhist Texts from Japan* (Oxford: Clarendon Press, 1881), p. 50.

18 Daisetz Teitaro Suzuki, *Manual of Zen Buddhism* (New York: Ballantine Books, 1974), p. 27.

19 Edward Conze, *Buddhist Wisdom*, 1st ed., Vintage Spiritual Classics (New York: Vintage Books, 2001), p. 113.

20 Bstan-dzin-rgya-mtsho, Dalai Lama XIV, and Jinpa, *Essence of the Heart Sutra*, pp. 130–31.

21 Thich Nhat Hanh and Annabel Laity, *The Other Shore: A New Translation of the Heart Sutra with Commentaries* (Berkeley: Parallax Press, 2017, Kindle ed.), pp. 1–2, 116.

22 Conze, *Buddhist Wisdom*, p. 113.

23 Red Pine, *The Heart Sutra: The Womb of Buddhas* (Washington, DC: Shoemaker and Hoard, 2004), p. 5

24 Donald S. Lopez Jr., "Inscribing the Bodhisattva's Speech: On the 'Heart Sūtra's' Mantra," *History of Religions* 29, no. 4 (1990): 360–61.

25 Kazuaki Tanahashi, *The Heart Sutra: A Comprehensive Guide to the Classic of Mahayana Buddhism* (Boston: Shambala, 2014), p. 7.

26 Fumimasa Fukui, *Hannya shingyō no sōgōteki kenkyū: Rekishi, shakai, shiryo* [A comprehensive study of the Heart Sutra: History, society, and materials] (Tokyo: Shunjūsha, 2000), pp. 530–45. The extra characters appear before the string 顛倒夢想.

27 Bstan-dzin-rgya-mtsho, Dalai Lama XIV, and Jinpa, *Essence of the Heart Sutra*, pp. 25–28,120. Robert E. Buswell Jr. and Donald S. Lopez Jr., *The Princeton Dictionary of Buddhism* (Princeton: Princeton University Press, 2014, Kindle ed.); see entry for "skandha."

28 Buswell and Lopez, *The Princeton Dictionary of Buddhism* (Kindle ed.). See entry for "dharmacakrapravartana."

29 In recent years, "Hinayana" seems to have fallen out of favor with many scholars because it has a slightly pejorative connotation. It means "The Little Wheel," and early adherents of the Mahayana, or "The Big Wheel" school of Buddhism, used it to

refer to, and distinguish themselves from, the older school.

30 Buswell and Lopez, *The Princeton Dictionary of Buddhism* (Kindle ed.). See entry for "Nāgārjuna."

31 Karl Brunnhölzl, *The Heart Attack Sutra: A New Commentary on the Heart Sutra* (Ithaca, NY: Snow Lion Publications, 2012), pp. 7–8.

32 Fukui Fumimasa, *Yoroppa no tōhōgaku to Hannya shingyō kenkyū no rekishi* [Oriental studies in Europe and the history of research on the Heart Sutra] (Tokyo: Goyō Shobō, 2008), pp. 306–22.

33 Mark Blum, email to author, 2 September 2020. See also Mark Blum, vol. ed., *Selected Works of Daisetsu Suzuki, Vol. 4: Buddhist Studies* (Oakland: University of California Press, 2020), pp. 181–85.

34 Charles A. Muller, ed., and Jimmy Yu, "Digital Dictionary of Buddhism," http://www.buddhism-dict.net/cgi-bin/xpr-ddb.pl?q=空.

35 Buswell and Lopez, *The Princeton Dictionary of Buddhism* (Kindle ed.). See entry for "śūnyatā."

36 Daisetz Teitaro Suzuki and Christmas Humphreys, *Essays in Zen Buddhism. Ser. 3.* (London: Ryder, 1953), pp. 203–5.

37 Tanahashi, *The Heart Sutra.* See "A New Translation," p. 7.

38 Beal, "The Páramitá-Hṛidaya Sútra, or, in Chinese, 'Moho-pō-ye-po-lo-mih-to-sin-king,' i.e., 'The Great Páramitá Heart Sútra,'" pp. 25–28.

39 Buswell and Lopez, *The Princeton Dictionary of Buddhism* (Kindle ed.). See entry for "annuttarasamyaksambohdi."

40 Xu Xu, *Bird Talk and Other Stories by Xu Xu: Modern Tales of a Chinese Romantic,* trans. Frederik H. Green (Berkeley: Stone Bridge Press, 2020), p. 139.

41 Mark Blum, email to author, 19 November 2017.

42 Ian Johnson, "Is a Buddhist Group Changing China? Or Is China Changing It?," *New York Times*, 24 June 2017.

43 Profile at https://kanho.info/profile (accessed 4 October 2019). Emails from Ogawa Mayumi of Yūgen Creations to author, 28 November 2019 and 2 December 2019.

44   Ian Johnson, "Finding Zen and Book Contracts in Beijing,"
      New York Books, 29 May 2012, https://www.nybooks.com/
      daily/2012/05/29/zen-book-contracts-bill-porter-beijing/.
      Clare Morin, "My Life: Red Pine," *South China Morning Post*, 3 May
      2014, https://www.scmp.com/magazines/post-magazine/
      article/1495760/my-life-red-pine (accessed 16 December 2019).
      Also email communications with Bill Porter.

45   Buswell and Lopez, *The Princeton Dictionary of Buddhism* (Kindle
      ed.). See entry for "Kumārajīva."

46   Mu Soeng Sunim, *Heart of the Universe: Exploring the Heart Sutra*
      (Somerville, MA: Wisdom Publications, 2010), pp. 3–4.

47   Watanabe Shōgo, *Hannya shingyō: tekusuto, shisō, bunka* [The
      Heart Sutra: Texts, thought, culture] (Tokyo: Daihōrinkaku,
      2009), pp. 56–60.

48   Xuanzang, Bianji, and Rongxi Li, *The Great Tang Dynasty Record
      of the Western Regions* (Berkeley: Numata Center for Buddhist
      Translation and Research, 1996), p. 15.

49   Huili, Jung-hsi Li, and Yancong, *A Biography of the Tripiṭaka
      Master of the Great Ci'en Monastery of the Great Tang Dynasty*, BDK
      English Tripitaka (Berkeley: Numata Center for Buddhist Transla-
      tion and Research, 1995), p. 7.

50   Ibid., p. 24.

51   Ibid., pp. 26–27.

52   Robert Malcolm Gay, *The College Book of Verse, 1250–1925* (Boston,
      New York, and elsewhere: Houghton Mifflin, 1927), pp. 362–63.

53   Huili, Li, and Yancong, *A Biography of the Tripiṭaka Master*, pp.
      38–41. Xuanzang, Bianji, and Li, *The Great Tang Dynasty Record of
      the Western Regions*, pp. 17–20.

54   Huili, Li, and Yancong, *A Biography of the Tripiṭaka Master*, pp. 68,
      90–97.

55   Harada Wasō, *"Hannya shingyō" seiritsu shiron: Daijō bukkyō to mik-
      kyō no kōsaro* [Theories on the development of the Heart Sutra:
      At the crossroads of Mahayana and Esoteric Buddhism] (Tokyo:
      Daizō Shuppan, 2010), pp. 34–36. Dan Lusthaus, *The Heart Sutra*

in Chinese Yogacara: Some Comparative Comments on the Heart Sutra Commentaries of Wonchuk and Kuei-Chi, vol. 3 (Seoul, Korea: International Association for Buddhist Thought and Culture, 2003), pp. 63–64.

56   Xuanzang, Bianji, and Li, *The Great Tang Dynasty Record of the Western Regions*, p. 349.

57   Huili, Li, and Yancong, *A Biography of the Tripiṭaka Master*, pp. 163–76.

58   Ibid., pp. 17, 26, 194–201.

59   Red Pine, *The Heart Sutra: The Womb of Buddhas*, p. 180.

60   For an account of how Empress Wu came to be notorious, see Jonathan Clements, *Wu: The Chinese Empress Who Schemed, Seduced, and Murdered Her Way to Become a Living God* (Stroud, Glos.: Sutton Publishing, 2007).

61   Huili, Li, and Yancong, *A Biography of the Tripiṭaka Master*, p. 305. Tsang Hsüan and Deva Devahuti, *The Unknown Hsüan-Tsang* (Delhi: Oxford University Press, 2001), p. 154.

62   Huili, Li, and Yancong, *A Biography of the Tripiṭaka Master*, p. 333.

63   Lusthaus, *The Heart Sutra in Chinese Yogacara*, vol. 3, pp. 64–65.

64   "Fangshan shijing <Xinjing> Kanke yanjiu chengguo fabu: Bei renwei shi xiancun zuizao banben, wei xuanzang suo" [Publication of results of research into Fangshan stele of the "Heart Sutra" considered to be earliest existing version by Xuanzang], *Xinhuanet*, http://www.xinhuanet.com/politics/2016-09/25/c_129297850.htm (accessed 6 June 2019). Jayarava Attwood, "Xuanzang's Relationship to the Heart Sūtra in Light of the Fangshan Stele," *Journal of Chinese Buddhist Studies* 32 (2019): 1–30.

65   Dharma Drum Mountain, http://www.dharmadrum.org/content/news/view.aspx?sn=1135 (accessed 24 November 2019).

66   For more information on the relationship between the series and *Journey to the West*, see Derek Padula's massive seven-volume work, *Dragon Ball Culture*: Derek Padula, *Dragon Ball Culture, Volume 1: Origin* (N.p.: Derek Padula, 2016).

67   Cheng'en Wu and Anthony C. Yu, *The Journey to the West. Volume I* (Chicago: University of Chicago Press, 2012, Kindle ed.), pp. 389–90.

68   Aurel Stein, *Sand-Buried Ruins of Khotan Personal Narrative of a Journey of Archaeological and Geographical Exploration in Chinese Turkestan; with Map* (London: Hurst, 1904), http://catalog. hathitrust.org/Record/100553932. pp. xxi, 231.

69   Aurel Stein and Archaeological Survey of India, *Ruins of Desert Cathay; Personal Narrative of Explorations in Central Asia and Westernmost China*, vol. 2 (London: Macmillan and Company, 1912), p. 171.

70   Neville Agnew et al., *Cave Temples of Dunhuang: Buddhist Art on China's Silk Road* (Los Angeles: Getty Conservation Institute, 2016), p. 10.

71   Interview by author, 21 October 2019, Piedmont, CA.

72   Ibid.

73   *The Holy Bible: Revised Standard Version* (New York: Thomas Nelson and Sons, 1952), p. iii.

74   Robert E. Buswell, *Chinese Buddhist Apocrypha* (Honolulu: University of Hawaii Press, 1990), p. 1.

75   Ibid., p. 5

76   Jan Nattier, "The Heart Sūtra: A Chinese Apocryphal Text?," *Journal of the International Association of Buddhist Studies* 15, no. 2 (1992): 154.

77   John R. McRae, "Ch'an Commentaries on the Heart Sūtra: Preliminary Inferences on the Permutation of Chinese Buddhism," *Journal of the International Association of Buddhist Studies* 11, no. 2 (1988): 87.

78   Also known in long-winded Sanskrit as the *Pañcaviṃśatisāhasrikāprajñāpāramitāsūtra*.

79   Peter Hopkirk, *Foreign Devils on the Silk Road: The Search for the Lost Cities and Treasures of Chinese Central Asia* (London: Murray, 1980), pp. 45–57, 98–109

80   Jayarava Attwood, "The Buddhas of the Three Times and the

Chinese Origins of the Heart Sutra," *Journal of the Oxford Centre for Buddhist Studies* (2018): 10.

81   Tanahashi, *The Heart Sutra: A Comprehensive Guide to the Classic of Mahayana Buddhism*, pp.73–89.

82   Red Pine, *The Heart Sutra: The Womb of Buddhas*, pp. 22–27.

83   Ji Yun, "Is the Heart Sūtra an Apocryphal Text? A Re-Examination [Trans by Chin Shih-Foong]," *Singapore Journal of Buddhist Studies* 4 (2017): 9–113.

84   Jayarava Attwood to *Jayarava's Raves*, 18 June 2018, http://jayarava.blogspot.com/2018/06/review-of-ji-yuns-is-heart-sutra.html.

85   Digital Library and Museum of Buddhist Studies, http://buddhism.lib.ntu.edu.tw/DLMBS/website/latestnewsdetail.jsp?id=5167 (accessed 22 July 2019).

86   Fukui, *Hannya shingyō no sōgōteki kenkyū: Rekishi, shakai, shiryo*, p. 29.

87   Henry Shiu (邵頌雄), emails to author between 31 July 2019 and 16 September 2019.

88   Fukui Fumimasa, *Hannya shingyō no rekishiteki kenkyū* (1987), pp. 22–23, 207–9.

89   Jan Nattier, "Jan Nattier-cho: Hannya shingyō wa chūgoku gikyō ka?" [Jan Nattier's "The Heart Sūtra: A Chinese Apocryphal Text?"], trans. Kudō Noriyuki and Fukita Takamichi, *Sankō bunka kenkyūjo nenpō* [Annual of the Sanko Research Institute for the Studies of Buddhism], 37 (2007): 17–83.

90   Fukui, *Hannya shingyō no sōgōteki kenkyū: Rekishi, shakai, shiryo*, pp. 561–62.

91   Aragane Nobuharu, "Gantō shōgyōjo konryū no kei" [Construction of the "Wild Goose Pagoda Sacred Preface"], *Memoirs of Beppu University* 34 (1993/01): 9–31.

92   Fukui, *Hannya shingyō no sōgōteki kenkyū*, pp. 27–28, 562.

93   Nattier, "The Heart Sūtra: A Chinese Apocryphal Text?," pp. 180–81.

94   Fukui, *Hannya shingyō no sōgōteki kenkyū*, pp. 10, 554.

95 Harada Wasō, "Bonpon 'shōhon-Hannya shingyō' wayaku" [A Japanese translation of the Sanskrit short recension of the Heart Sutra], *Mikkyō Bunka*, no. 209 (2002): 34–37.

96 Nattier, "Jan Nattier-cho: Hannya shingyō wa chūgoku gikyō ka?," pp. 81–83.

97 Watanabe, *Hannya Shingyō: Tekusuto, shisō, bunka*, pp. 11–14.

98 Watanabe Shōgo, "Hannya shingyō seiritsuronjosetsu: Maka hannyaharamitsu daimyōjukyō to daihon hannyakyō no kankei wo chūshin to shite" [A study on the formation of the Prajñāpāramitā-Hṛdaya-Sūtra]," *Bukkyōgaku* [Journal of Buddhist Studies] 31 (1991): 41–86.

99 Harada, *"Hannya shingyō" seiritsu shiron: Daijō bukkyō to mikkyō no kōsaro*, pp. 430–31.

100 Ishii Kōsei, "'Hannya shingyō' wo meguru shomondai" [Doubts about Jan Nattier's theory of Xuanzang's creation of the Heart Sutra], *Indogaku bukkyōgaku kenkyū* [Journal of Indian and Buddhist Studies] 64, no. 1 (2015): 499.

101 Jeffry Kotyk, "Chinese State and Buddhist Historical Sources on Xuanzang: Historicity and the *Daci'en si sanzang fashi zhuan* 大慈恩寺三藏法師傳," *T'oung Pao* 105 (2019): 513–44.

102 Jan Nattier, "Response to Fukui Fumimasa, '*Hannya shingyō no kenkyūshi—Genkon no mondaiten*,' Published in *Bukkyōgaku* No. 36, December, 1994, pp. 79–99)" (unpublished paper, 1995).

103 Jan Nattier, email to author, 2 November 2019.

104 Ibid.

105 Watanabe, *Hannya shingyō: Tekusuto, shiso, bunka*, p. 14.

106 United States Central Intelligence Agency, "'Japan,' *The World Factbook*," https://www.cia.gov/library/publications/resources/the-world-factbook/attachments/summaries/JA-summary.pdf. (accessed 21 December 2019).

107 Allan G. Grapard, "Shinto," in *Kodansha Encyclopedia of Japan* (Tokyo and New York: Kodansha, 1983), vol. 7, p. 127.

108 Nattier, "The Heart Sūtra: A Chinese Apocryphal Text?," p. 153.

109 Studio IDU and Edit Z, "Kairyuō-ji no sugoi tokoro" (Nara:

Kairyuō-ji, 2016), pp. 1–8, and "Genbō-san no sugoi tokoro" (Nara: Kairyuō-ji, 2017), pp. 1–8.

110 Watanabe, *Hannya shingyō: Tekusuto, shisō, bunka*, pp. 282–84, 302–4.

111 Ibid., pp. 282–92, 310–16.

112 Daigaku Rummé email to author, 29 October 2019.

113 Yamada Hōin, "Tameshite goran 'kaku kudoku,' 'tonaeru koyō,' 'shakyō no kokoro,' 'dokkyō no susume'" [Try it. In praise of the merits of writing it; the advantages of chanting it; the spirit of copying and reading it], in *Akarui akirame: "Hannya shingyō" nyūmon* [Positive Surrender: An Introduction to the Heart Sutra], *President+Plus* 48, no. 34 (25 December 2010): 32–41.

114 Watanabe Shōgo, *Etoki Hannya shingyō: Hannya shingyō no bunkateki kenkyū* [Explaining the Heart Sutra in pictures: Cultural studies in the Heart Sutra] (Tokyo: Nonburusha, 2012), pp. 21–22, 32, 93–101.

115 Yakushiji Kanho Kissaquo Official Website, https://kanho.info/profile (accessed 4 October 2019). Emails from Ogawa Mayumi of Yūgen Creations to author, 28 November 2019 and 2 December 2019.

116 Ryūshō Shinpo, "Shakyō no susume," in *Hannya shingyō wo toku* [Explaining the Heart Sutra] (Tokyo: Daihōrinkaku, 2005), pp. 149–59.

117 Kubota Shirō and Sakura Sōgorō, *Bushū iwatsuki genjōto monogatari* [The story of the bushū iwatsuki Xuanzang pagoda] (N.p.: Genjōsanzōhōshi no Sato Zukuri Jikkōiinkai, 2010), pp. 12–28.

118 Ibid.

119 Yakushi-ji, *Genjō sanzō to yakushiji* [Xuanzang and Yakushi-ji temple] (Nara: Hossōshū Daihonzan Yakushiji, 2015), pp. 98–100.

120 Damien Keown et al., *A Dictionary of Buddhism* (Oxford: Oxford University Press, 2003, Kindle ed.), p.110.

121 Yakushi-ji, *Genjō sanzō to yakushiji*, pp. 142–43.

122 Masahirō Mori and Charles S. Terry, *The Buddha in the Robot: A Robot Engineer's Thoughts on Science and Religion* (Tokyo: Kosei

Publishing, 1985), pp. 7–9. Frederik L. Schodt, *Inside the Robot Kingdom: Japan, Mechatronics, and the Coming Robotopia* (Tokyo: Kodansha International, 1988), pp. 207–10.

123 Mori and Terry, *The Buddha in the Robot,* p. 8.

124 Mori Masahirō, "*Kaichō shūnin no goaisatsu*" [Words from the new chairman], *Journal of the Robotics Society of Japan,* 2 February 1987, p. 3 (translation by the author).

125 Mori Masahirō, "Jizai kenkyūsho no kokoro" [The spirit of the Mukta Institute], in *Hannya shingyō wo toku* [Explaining the Heart Sutra] (Tokyo: Daihōrinkaku, 2005), pp. 117–19 (translation by the author).

126 Interview with Matsubara Sueo, 27 February 1986.

127 Schodt, *Inside the Robot Kingdom*, pp. 208–9.

128 Studied extensively by Assistant Professor Courtney R. Brunz of Douane University's Asian Religions department.

129 Ukai Hidenori , "'Ichioku en no robotto Kannon' MINDAR no nerai" [Goal of the 100 million yen robot Kannon, MINDAR]," *President On-line*, https://president.jp/articles/-/28134 (27 March 2019).

130 Ogawa Kohei, email to author, 17 October 2019.

131 Gotō Tenshō, "Andoroido Kannon MINDAR" [The android Kannon MINDAR], *Chūnichi,* 28 May 2019.

132 Honda Dōryū , email to author, 8 October 2019.

133 Kōdai-ji and Yuki Warae, *Manga andoroido Kannon ga hannya shingyō wo katarihajimeta* [Manga: The android Kannon has begun to talk about the Heart Sutra] (Kyoto: Kamogawa Shuppan, 2019).

134 Donald S. Lopez Jr., *Elaborations on Emptiness: Uses of the "Heart Sutra"* (Princeton: Princeton University Press, 1996), pp. 1–2.

135 Lafcadio Hearn, *Kwaidan: Stories and Studies of Strange Things* (Boston and New York: Houghton, Mifflin, 1904), pp. 16–17.

136 "Hakushi bio," https://www.wwe.com/superstars/hakushi (accessed 23 December 2019).

137 "Kajino Shingichū, 'Hannya shingyō' tonae jikan shōhi, jimin Tanikawa-shi" [While debating casinos, Liberal Democratic

Party's Tanikawa recites the Heart Sutra to use up his time], *Asahi Shinbun* (Digital), 5 December 2016, https://www.asahi. com/articles/ASJD556HXJD5UTFK00C.html (accessed 16 December 2019). Haruo Isono et al., "2d2-3 Measurement of Cerebral Blood Flow When Person Is Transcribing, Silent Reading and Chanting the 'Hannya shingyō,'" *Japanese Journal of Ergonomics* 50 (2014): S298-S299.

138 Miura Jun, *Autodoa Hannya shingyō* (Tokyo: Gentosha, 2007), pp. 1–7.

139 Ikeda Masuo and Myūjiamu Paramita, *Hannya shingyō: Ikeda Masuo no sekai* [The Heart Sutra: The world of Ikeda Masuo] (Komono-machi: Okada Bunka Zaidan Paramita Myūjiamu, 2006), pp. 136–38.

140 Harada, *"Hannya shingyō" seiritsu shiron: Daijō bukkyō to mikkyō no kōsaro*, pp. 1–2.

141 Fukui, *Yoroppa no tohogaku to Hannya shingyō kenkyū no rekishi*, pp. 330–32.

142 Edward Conze, "Text, Sources, and Bibliography of the Prajñā-pāramitā-Hṛdaya," *Journal of the Royal Asiatic Society of Great Britain and Ireland*, no. 1 (1948): 48.

143 Nanba Mitsusada, "Eigo de yomeba, konna ni wakariyasui eiyaku Hannya Shingyō" [If you read it in English, the Heart Sutra is so easy to understand], in *Akarui akirame "Hannya Shingyō nyūmon"* [Positive Surrender: An Introduction to the Heart Sutra], *President+Plus* 48, no. 34 (25 December 2010), pp. 82–88.

144 Suzuki and Humphreys, *Essays in Zen Buddhism. Ser. 3.*, p. 203.

145 Edward Conze, *Buddhist Texts through the Ages: Newly Transl. From the Original Pali, Sanskrit, Chinese, Tibetan, Japanese and Apabhramsa: Under the Auspices of the Royal India, Pakistan and Ceylon Society* (Oxford: Oneworld Publications, 1995), p. 152.

146 Thich Nhat Hanh and Peter Levitt, *The Heart of Understanding: Commentaries on the Prajñaparamita Heart Sutra* (Berkeley: Parallax Press, 2009), pp. 1–2.

147 Nanba, "Eigo de yomeba, konna ni wakariyasui eiyaku Hannya

Shingyō," pp. 85–88. Nhat and Laity, *The Other Shore: A New Translation of the Heart Sutra with Commentaries*, pp. 23–26.

148 Daigaku Rummé, email to author, 29 October 2019.

149 Paula Kane Robinson Arai and Robert A. F. Thurman, eds., *Painting Enlightenment: Healing Visions of the Heart Sutra* (Boulder, CO: Shambhala, 2019), p. i.

150 Ibid., p. 33.

151 Mu Soeng Sunim, *Heart Sutra: Ancient Buddhist Wisdom in the Light of Quantum Reality* (Cumberland, RI: Primary Point Press, 1991), p. ii.

152 Nadja Van Ghelue, *The Heart Sutra in Calligraphy: A Visual Appreciation of the Perfection of Wisdom* (Berkeley: Stone Bridge Press, 2009), pp. 12–13.

153 Daigaku Rummé, email to author, 31 October 2019.

Select Bibliography

Agnew, Neville, Marcia Reed, Tevvy Ball, Getty Conservation Institute, Getty Research Institute, and Dunhuang Yan Jiu Yuan (China). *Cave Temples of Dunhuang: Buddhist Art on China's Silk Road.* Los Angeles: Getty Conservation Institute, 2016.

Akagi Takayuki. "Genjō yaku 'Hannya Shingyō' no denrai to ryūfu" [On the Introduction of Xuanzang's Version of Prajnaparamita-Hṛdaya into Japan and Its Circulation]. *Shikan* 172 (2015): 1–21.

Aragane Nobuharu. "Gantō shōgyōjo konryū no kei" [Construction of the "Wild Goose Pagoda Sacred Preface"]. *Memoirs of Beppu University* 34 (1993/01): 9–31.

Arai, Paula Kane Robinson, and Robert A. F. Thurman. *Painting Enlightenment: Healing Visions of the Heart Sutra.* 1st ed. Boulder, CO: Shambhala, 2019.

Attwood, Jayarava. "The Buddhas of the Three Times and the Chinese Origins of the Heart Sutra." *Journal of Chinese Buddhist Studies* 15 (2018): 9–27.

———. "Review of Ji Yun's 'Is the Heart Sutra an Apocryphal Text? A Re-Examination.'" In *Jayarava's Raves*, 2018.

———. "Xuanzang's Relationship to the Heart Sūtra in Light of the Fangshan Stele." *Journal of Chinese Buddhist Studies* 32 (2019): 1–30.

Beal, Samuel. *A Catena of Buddhist Scriptures from the Chinese.* London: Trübner, 1871.

———. "The Páramitá-Hṛidaya Sútra, or, in Chinese, 'Moho-pô-ye-po-lo-mih-to-sin-king,' i.e., 'The Great Páramitá Heart Sútra.'" *Journal of the Royal Asiatic Society of Great Britain and Ireland, New Series* 1, no. 1/2 (1865): 25–28.

Brunnhölzl, Karl. *The Heart Attack Sutra: A New Commentary on the Heart Sutra.* Ithaca, N.Y.: Snow Lion Publications, 2012.

Bstan-dzin-rgya-mtsho, Dalai Lama XIV, and Thupten Jinpa. *Essence of the Heart Sutra: The Dalai Lama's Heart of Wisdom Teachings.* 1st paperback ed. Boston: Wisdom Publications, 2005.

Buswell Jr., Robert E. *Chinese Buddhist Apocrypha.* Honolulu: University of Hawaii Press, 1990.

_____ and Donald S. Lopez Jr. *The Princeton Dictionary of Buddhism.* Princeton: Princeton University Press, 2014. Kindle ed.

Clements, Jonathan. *A Brief History of China: Dynasty, Revolution, and Transformation.* North Clarendon, VT: Tuttle Publishing, 2019.

_____. *An Armchair Traveller's History of The Silk Road.* London: Haus Publishing, 2014.

--------. *Wu: The Chinese Empress Who Schemed, Seduced, and Murdered Her Way to Become a Living God.* Stroud, Glos.: Sutton Publishing, 2007.

Conze, Edward. *Buddhist Texts through the Ages: Newly Transl. From the Original Pali, Sanskrit, Chinese, Tibetan, Japanese and Apabhramsa: Under the Auspices of the Royal India, Pakistan and Ceylon Society.* Oxford: Cassirer, 1954.

———. *Buddhist Wisdom: Containing the Diamond Sutra and the Heart Sutra.* Vintage Spiritual Classics. 1st ed. New York: Vintage Books, 2001.

_____. "The Heart Sutra Explained I." *The Middle Way: Journal of the Buddhist Society* 30, no. 3, 1955.

_____. "The Heart Sutra Explained II." *The Middle Way: Journal of the Buddhist Society* 30, no. 4, 1956.

———. "Prajnaparamita-Hrdaya." *The Middle Way: Journal of the Buddhist Society* 20 no. 5, 1946.

———. *The Short Prajñaparamita Texts.* London: Luzac and Co., 1973.

———. "Text, Sources, and Bibliography of the Prajñāpāramitā-Hṛdaya." *Journal of the Royal Asiatic Society of Great Britain and Ireland*, no. 1 (1948): 33–51.

———. *Thirty Years of Buddhist Studies: Selected Studies*. Oxford: Cassirer, 1967.

Devahuti, D. *The Unknown Hsüan-Tsang*. New Delhi and New York: Oxford University Press, 2001.

Edit Z, Studio IDU. "Genbō-san no sugoi tokoro" [Awesome facts about Genbō-san]. Nara: Kairyūō-ji, 2017.

———. "Kairyūō-ji no sugoi tokoro" [Awesome facts about Kairyūō]. Nara: Kairyūō-ji, 2016.

Fukui Fumimasa. *Hannya shingyō no rekishiteki kenkyū* [Historical Studies of the Buddhist scripture]. Tokyo: Shunjūsha,1987.

———. *Hannya shingyō no sōgōteki kenkyū: Rekishi, shakai, shiryo* [A comprehensive study of the Heart Sutra: History, society, and materials]. Tokyo: Shunjūsha, 2000.

———. *Yoroppa no tōhōgaku to Hannya shingyō kenkyū no rekishi* [Oriental studies in Europe and the history of research on the Heart Sutra]. Tokyo; Goyō Shobō, 2008.

Gen'yū Sōkyū. *Gendaigoyaku Hannya shingyō* [A modern translation of the Heart Sutra]. Tokyo: Chikuma Shobō, 2006.

Ginsberg, Allen. *Mind Breaths: Poems, 1972–1977*. The Pocket Poets Series. San Francisco: City Lights Books, 1977.

_____. "The Vomit of a Mad Tyger." *Shambhala Sun* 2, no. 6 (1994).

Goddard, Dwight. *A Buddhist Bible: The Favorite Scriptures of the Zen Sect History of Early Zen Buddhism, Self-Realisation of Noble Wisdom, the Diamond Sutra, the Prajna Paramita Sutra, the Sutra of the Sixth Patriarch*. Thetford, VT: E. P. Dutton and Co., 1932.

Goodyear, Dana. "Zen Master: Gary Snyder and the Art of Life." *The New Yorker*, 20 October 2008: 66–75.

Hakuin. *Zen Words for the Heart: Hakuin's Commentary on the Heart Sutra*. Translated by Norman Waddell. Boston: Shambhala, 1996.

Halper, Jon, and Sierra Club. *Gary Snyder: Dimensions of a Life*. San Francisco: Sierra Club Books, 1991.

Hanh, Thich Naht, and Annabel Laity. *The Other Shore: A New Translation of the Heart Sutra with Commentaries.* Berkeley: Parallax Press, 2017. Kindle ed.

Hanh, Thich Naht, and Peter Levitt. *The Heart of Understanding: Commentaries on the Prajñaparamita Heart Sutra.* Berkeley: Parallax Press, 2009.

Harada Wasō. "Bonpon 'shōhon-Hannya shingyō' wayaku" [A Japanese translation of the Sanskrit short recension of the Heart Sutra]. *Mikkyō Bunka*, no. 209 (2002): L17–L62.

———. *"Hannya shingyō" seiritsu shiron: Daijō bukkyō to mikkyō no kōsaro* [Theories on the development of the Heart Sutra: At the crossroads of Mahayana and Esoteric Buddhism]. Tokyo: Daizō Shuppan, 2010.

Hearn, Lafcadio. *Kwaidan: Stories and Studies of Strange Things.* Boston and New York: Houghton, Mifflin, 1904.

Hopkirk, Peter. *Foreign Devils on the Silk Road: The Search for the Lost Cities and Treasures of Chinese Central Asia.* London: Murray, 1980.

Hsüan-Tsang and Deva Devahuti. *The Unknown Hsüan-Tsang.* Delhi: Oxford University Press, 2001.

Hotori Rishō. *"Prajñāpāramitā Hṛdaya no seiritsushiron* [An attempt to explain the formation of the Prajñāpāramitā Hṛdaya]." *Indogaku bukkyōgaku kenkyū* [Journal of Indian and Buddhist Studies] 58, no. 2 (2010): 975–70.

Huìfēng Shì. *Apocryphal Treatment for Conze's Heart Problems: "Non-Attainment," "Apprehension," and "Mental Hanging" in the Prajñāpāramitā Hṛdaya* 6, Oxford: Oxford Centre for Buddhist Studies, 2014.

Huili, Jung-hsi Li, and Yancong. *A Biography of the Tripiṭaka Master of the Great Ci'en Monastery of the Great Tang Dynasty.* BDK English Tripitaka. Berkeley: Numata Center for Buddhist Translation and Research, 1995.

Ikeda Masuo and Paramita Museum. *Hannya shingyō: Ikeda Masuo no sekai* [The Heart Sutra: The world of Ikeda Masuo] Komonomachi, Mie: Okada Bunka Zaidan Paramita Myūjiamu, 2006.

Ishii Kōsei. "'Hannya shingyō' wo meguru shomondai" [Doubts about Jan Nattier's theory of Xuanzang's creation of the Heart Sutra]. *Indogaku bukkyōgaku kenkyū* [Journal of Indian and Buddhist Studies] 64, no. 1 (2015): 499–92.

Ji Yun. "Is the Heart Sūtra an Apocryphal Text?—A Re-Examination [Trans by Chin Shih-Foong]." *Singapore Journal of Buddhist Studies* 4 (2017): 9–113.

Johnson, Ian. "Finding Zen and Book Contracts in Beijing." *New York Review of Books*, 29 May 2012. https://www.nybooks.com/daily/2012/05/29/zen-book-contracts-bill-porter-beijing/. Accessed 16 December 2019.

———. "Is a Buddhist Group Changing China? Or Is China Changing It?" *New York Times*, 24 June 2017: A1.

Keown, Damien, Stephen Hodge, Paola Tinti, and Charles Jones. *A Dictionary of Buddhism.* Oxford: Oxford University Press, 2003. Kindle ed.

Kerouac, Jack. *Some of the Dharma.* New York: Viking, 1997.

Kōdai-ji and Yuki Warae. *Manga andoroido Kannon ga hannya shingyō wo katarihajimeta* [Manga: An android Kannon has begun to talk about the Heart Sutra]. Kyoto: Kamogawa Publishing, 2019.

Kotyk, Jeffrey. "Chinese State and Buddhist Historical Sources on Xuanzang: Historicity and the Daci'en si sanzang fashi zhuan 大慈恩寺三藏法師傳." *T'oung Pao* 105 (2020): 513–44.

Kubota Shirō and Sakura Sōgorō. *Bushū iwatsuki genjōto monogatari* [Story of the Bushū Iwatsuki Xuanzang pagoda]. N.p.: Genjōsanzōhōshi no Sato Zukuri Jikkōiinkai, 2010.

Kuiji, Heng-ching Shih, and Dan Lusthaus. *A Comprehensive Commentary on the Heart Sutra (Prajñāpāramita-Hṛdaya-Sūtra).* Berkeley: Numata Center for Buddhist Translation and Research, 2001.

Kyger, Joanne. *The Japan and India Journals, 1960–1964.* New York: Nightboat Books, 2016.

Lancaster, Lewis R., Luis O. Gomez, and Edward Conze. *Prajnaparamita and Related Systems: Studies in Honor of Edward Conze.* Berkeley Buddhist Studies Series. Berkeley: Regents of the University of

California, 1977.

Lancaster, Lewis R., and Sung-bae Park. *The Korean Buddhist Canon: A Descriptive Catalogue.* Berkeley: University of California Press, 1979.

Lopez Jr., Donald S. *The Heart Sutra Explained: Indian and Tibetan Commentaries.* Albany: State University of New York Press, 1988.

_____. "Inscribing the Bodhisattva's Speech: On the 'Heart Sūtra's' Mantra." *History of Religions* 29, no. 4 (1990): 351–72.

--------. *Elaborations on Emptiness: Uses of the "Heart Sutra."* Princeton: Princeton University Press, 1996.

Lusthaus, Dan. *The Heart Sutra in Chinese Yogacara: Some Comparative Comments on the Heart Sutra Commentaries of Wonchuk and Kuei-Chi.* Vol. 3. Seoul: International Association for Buddhist Thought and Culture, 2003.

McRae, John R. "Ch'an Commentaries on the Heart Sūtra: Preliminary Inferences on the Permutation of Chinese Buddhism." *Journal of the International Association of Buddhist Studies* 11, no. 2 (1988): 85–115.

Miura Jun. *Autodoa hannya shingyō* [Outdoor Heart Sutra]. Tokyo: Gentōsha, 2007.

Mori Masahiro. "Jizai kenkyūsho no kokoro" [The Spirit of the Mukta Institute]. In *Hannya shingyō wo toku* [Explaining the Heart Sutra]. Tokyo: Daihōrinkaku, 2005.

----------------. "'Chō': Hannya no 'sokuhi no ronri'" ["Ultra": "Logic of Affirmation in Negation." In *Prajñāpāramitā*]. *Journal of Japan Society of Mechanical Engineers* 95 (887) (1992): 902–5.

Mori Masahiro and Charles S. Terry. *The Buddha in the Robot: A Robot Engineer's Thoughts on Science and Religion.* Tokyo: Kosei Publishing, 1985.

Morin, Clare. "My Life: Red Pine." *South China Morning Post.* https://www.scmp.com/magazines/post-magazine/article/1495760/my-life-red-pine. Accessed 16 December 2019.

Muller, Charles A., ed. "Digital Dictionary of Buddhism." http://www.buddhism-dict.net/cgi-bin/xpr-ddb.pl?q=空.

Müller, Friedrich Max. *Buddhist Texts from Japan.* Oxford: Clarendon Press, 1881.

_____. "On Sanskrit Texts Discovered in Japan." *Journal of the Royal Asiatic Society of Great Britain and Ireland* 12, no. 2 (1880): 153–88.

Nakamura Hajime and Kino Kazuyoshi. *Hannya shingyō • Kongō hannyakyō* [The Heart Sutra and the Diamond Sutra]. 2017 ed. Tokyo: Iwanami Shoten, 2001.

Nattier, Jan. *A Guide to the Earliest Chinese Buddhist Translations: Texts from the Eastern Han and Three Kingdoms Periods.* Tokyo: International Research Institute for Advanced Buddhology, Soka University, 2008.

_____. "The Heart Sūtra: A Chinese Apocryphal Text?" *Journal of the International Association of Buddhist Studies* 15, no. 2 (31 December 1992): 153–223.

———. "Jan Nattier-cho: Hannya shingyō wa chūgoku gikyō ka?" [Jan Nattier's article, Is the Heart Sutra an apocryphal Chinese text?]. Translated by Kudō Noriyuki and Fukita Takamichi." *Sankō Bunka Kenkyūjo Nenpō* [Annual of The Sankō Research Institute for the Studies of Buddhism] 37 (26 March 2007): 17–83.

———. "Response to Fukui Fumimasa's 'Hannya shingyō no kenkyūshi—Genkon no mondaiten' (Published in *Bukkyōgaku* No. 36, December 1994, pp. 79–99)." Unpublished article, 1995.

Padula, Derek. *Dragon Ball Culture, Volume 1: Origin.* N.p.: Derek Padula, 2016.

Red Pine. *The Heart Sutra: The Womb of Buddhas.* Washington, DC: Shoemaker and Hoard, 2004.

Schodt, Frederik L. *Inside the Robot Kingdom Japan, Mechatronics, and the Coming Robotopia.* Tokyo and New York: Kodansha International, 1988.

Schumacher, Michael. *Dharma Lion: A Critical Biography of Allen Ginsberg.* 1st ed. New York: St. Martin's Press, 1992.

Shengyan. *There Is No Suffering: A Commentary on the Heart Sutra.* Elmhurst, NY: Dharma Drum, 2001.

Shinpo Ryūshō. "Shakyō no susume" [In praise of sutra-copying]. In

Hannya shingyō wo toku [Explaining the Heart Sutra]. Tokyo: Dai-hōrinkaku, 2005.

Snyder, Gary. *Turtle Island.* New York: New Directions, 1974, p. 66.

———. "Walking the Great Ridge Omine on the Diamond-Womb Trail." *Kyoto Journal* 25 (24 December 1993).

Stein, Aurel. *Sand-buried Ruins of Khotan: Personal Narrative of a Journey of Archaeological and Geographical Exploration in Chinese Turkestan; with map.* London: Hurst, 1904. http://catalog.hathitrust.org/Record/100553932.

——— and Archaeological Survey of India. *Ruins of Desert Cathay; Personal Narrative of Explorations in Central Asia and Westernmost China.* 2 vols. London: Macmillan and Company, 1912.

Stirling, Isabel. *Zen Pioneer: The Life and Works of Ruth Fuller Sasaki.* Emeryville, CA: Shoemaker and Hoard, 2006.

Sunim, Mu Soeng. *Heart of the Universe: Exploring the Heart Sutra.* Wisdom Publications, 2010.

———. *Heart Sutra: Ancient Buddhist Wisdom in the Light of Quantum Reality.* Cumberland, RI: Primary Point Press, 1991.

Suzuki, Daisetz Teitaro. *Manual of Zen Buddhism.* New York: Ballantine Books, 1974.

——— and Christmas Humphreys. *Essays in Zen Buddhism. Ser. 3.* London: Rider and Company, 1953.

------. *Selected Works of D. T. Suzuki, Volume 4: Buddhist Studies.* Series edited by Richard M. Jaffe; volume edited by Mark L. Blum. Oakland: University of California Press, 2020.

T'an Hsu. *The Prajna Paramita Heart Sutra, Translated from Sanskrit into Chinese by Tripitaka Master Hsuan Tsang, Commentary.* New York: Sutra Translation Committee of the U.S. and Canada, 2000.

Tanahashi, Kazuaki. *The Heart Sutra: A Comprehensive Guide to the Classic of Mahayana Buddhism.* Boston: Shambala, 2014.

Tanaka Taiken. "Gary Snyder to bukkyō: Jiin to no kankei ni tsuite" [Gary Snyder and Buddhism: The relationship with temples]. *Journal of the Institute for Zen Studies, Aichigakuin University* 11 (1982): 51–70.

Tatematsu Wahei. *Konji kindei hannya shingyō: Nihon saikō sumideraban* [Gold on dark blue Heart Sutra: Japan's oldest Sumidera edition]. Tokyo: Shōgakukan, 2002.

Tytell, John. *Naked Angels: Kerouac, Ginsberg, Burroughs.* New York: Grove Weidenfeld, 1991.

Van Ghelue, Nadja. *The Heart Sutra in Calligraphy: A Visual Appreciation of the Perfection of Wisdom.* Berkeley: Stone Bridge Press, 2009.

Wang Guohua. *Xinjing jian lin: Raozong yi[xinjing] shufayi shu* [The Heart Sutra wisdom path: The calligraphy of Rao Zong]. Hong Kong: Zhonghua shuju, 2016.

Warren, Henry Clarke. *Buddhism in Translations; Passages Selected from the Buddhist Sacred Books and Translated from the Original Pali into English.* Harvard Oriental Series 3. Cambridge, MA: Harvard University Press, 1915.

Watanabe Shōgo. *Etoki hannya shingyō: Hannya shingyō no bunkateki kenkyū* [Explaining the Heart Sutra in pictures: Cultural studies in the Heart Sutra]. Tokyo: Nonburusha, 2012.

———. *Hannya shingyō: Tekusuto, shisō, bunka* [The Heart Sutra: Texts, thought, culture]. Tokyo: Daihōrinkaku, 2009.

_____. "Hannya shingyō seiritsuron josetsu" [A study on the formation of the Prajñāpāramitā-Hṛdaya-Sūtra]." *Journal of Buddhist Studies* 31 (July 1991): 41–86.

Watts, Alan. *In My Own Way: An Autobiography, 1915–1965.* Novato, CA: New World Library, 2007.

Wayman, Alex, Edward Conze, Lewis R. Lancaster, and Luis O. Gómez. "Secret of the Heart Sutra." In *Prajñaparamita and Related Systems.* Berkeley Buddhist Studies Series. Berkeley: Regents of the University of California, 1977.

Wriggins, Sally Hovey. *The Silk Road Journey with Xuanzang.* Boulder, CO: Icon Editions, Westview Press, 2004.

Wu Cheng'en and Anthony C. Yu. *The Journey to the West. Volume I.* Chicago: Chicago University Press, 2012. Kindle ed.

Xuanzang, Bianji, and Rongxi Li. *The Great Tang Dynasty Record of the Western Regions.* Berkeley: Numata Center for Buddhist

Translation and Research, 1996.

Yaita Hideomi. "Hōryu-ji baiyō 'Hannya shingyō' shahon ni tsuite no hitohōkoku" [Report on the copy of the palm-leaf version of the Heart Sutra at Hōryū-ji]. *Chizan gakuhō* 50 (2001): A7–A16.

Yakushi-ji. *Genjō sanzō to yakushiji* [Xuanzang and Yakushi-ji temple]. Nara: Hossōshū Daihonzan Yakushi-ji, 2015.

Yamada Hōin. "Tameshite goran 'kaku kudoku,' 'tonaeru koyō,' 'shakyō no kokoro,' 'Dokkyō no susume'" [Try it. In praise of the merits of writing it; the advantages of chanting it; the spirit of copying and reading it]. In *Akarui akirame; 'Hannya shingyō' nyūmon, President+Plus* [Positive Surrender: An Introduction to the Heart Sutra], *President+Plus* 48, no. 34 (25 December 2010): 32–41.

Index